Now, Near, and Far

**The Kaufman Blogs,
2016-2024**

Now, Near, and Far

The Kaufman Blogs, 2016-2024

Ken Kaufman

Design and layout by Todd Douglas, Bold Yellow

ISBN: 979-8-9906213-0-5

Published by Leadership in Healthcare, Chicago, Illinois

This book is dedicated to all of my colleagues at

Kaufman Hall and to all of the hospital executives

I have had the honor to work with over my long career.

For me these daily interactions have been a lifelong

learning experience informing and making better

all of the work I have done. There really is no way to

adequately say "thank you" except to say "thank you."

Contents

Leadership

How Intense Should a Leader Be?

APRIL 17, 2024

Dawn Staley, head coach of the University of South Carolina's NCAA-tournament-winning women's basketball team, and Dan Hurley, head coach of the University of Connecticut's NCAA-tournament-winning men's basketball team, have something in common. In fact, they have a lot in common.

Most obviously, both coaches led their teams to victory from among 351 teams NCAA Division I teams and 68 teams in the men's and women's NCAA Division I tournaments.

Life Stories

It turns out that Staley and Hurley have a far deeper similarity—life stories that formed a foundation of the intensity that led to their recent championships.

Dawn Staley, 53, grew up in the projects of North Philadelphia and lived her life on the basketball courts there. This was a place where basketball wasn't just a thing, it was the only thing. A former high school classmate of Staley's (and later an NBA player) Bo Kimble put it this way: "It's the last bucket of the game and you drive to the basket, (and) they try to take your head off....If you survive on the court in Philly, you can survive anywhere, and Dawn is a product of that."[1]

Staley was a legendarily tough point guard at Dobbins Tech High School. Under her leadership on the court, Dobbins won three consecutive Philadelphia Public League championships. As a senior, Staley was named *USA Today*'s National High School Player of the Year.

Staley brought her Philly intensity and her Philly success not only to South Carolina but to her efforts to lift people of color everywhere. Marilyn Stephens, another product of Philly basketball and a basketball legend at Temple University, says of Staley, "It shows how a young girl…can come out of the projects and have such an influence on the world."

The grit of Philly is a close match for the grit of Jersey City, hometown of UConn head coach Dan Hurley. Hurley, 51, grew up in a family that lived and breathed basketball—and frequently breathed fire as well. As head coach of St. Anthony High School, Hurley's father, Bob Hurley, Sr., was often described as flammable. He led his team to an almost unimaginable 26 state championships in 39 years. Dan was a star on the St. Anthony team, as was his brother, Bob, Jr., with whom Dan battled in furious one-on-one games on the family driveway. As a player, Dan Hurley was described as "an in-your-face point guard," who "often looked pissed-off."[2]

At a recent press conference, Hurley said in his trademark Jersey accent, "I'm…a worse version of (my dad)…and I'm coming for him." One columnist called Hurley "a throwback to the days when college basketball coaches didn't seem so corporate, publicly beefed with each other, and told you exactly how good they thought they were."[3]

Would Staley-Style or Hurley-Style Leadership Play in Business?

Both Staley and Hurley bring an intensity to their workplace that is amazing to behold. Watching this on television, some of us love the intensity. Others probably say, "These two are over the top." Yet this level of intensity has resulted in two extraordinarily competitive NCAA championships.

Which leads me to these questions: Does this type of intensity transfer in any way to complex, large, corporate-style organizations? Would a Dawn Staley-style or Dan Hurley-style leader even be tolerated in a corporate environment today? Are some elements of their intensity transferable while others are not?

Lacking a definitive answer, let me advance a few opinions based on my decades of observing and interacting with corporate and hospital leaders.

A Focus on Goals

In my mind, some characteristics that Staley and Hurley demonstrate not only transfer to a corporate environment but are crucial to effective leadership. The intensity to be successful, to have a single goal in mind, to articulate that goal, and to insist that the organization manage to that goal and not stray from it—that is absolutely transferable. Hospital organizations of size and complexity are unfathomably difficult to lead and to manage today. There is no way to achieve the success that a company like that is striving for unless everybody in the organization understands the goals they are working toward.

"My Way or the Highway"

Staley and Hurley have the reputation as being "my way or the highway" style of leaders. Although this approach has fallen out of favor among business leaders, perhaps an aspect of it still applies. In the best sporting environments, in the environments where success is achieved on a regular basis, there are not multiple agendas. In some organizations, multiple personalities are tolerated, but not multiple agendas. At Hurley's place and at Staley's place, there is only one agenda. That's their agenda. If a player starts questioning the agenda, that player would be invited to hit the transfer portal.

In large corporate organizations, there are so many agendas—profit, innovation, competitive dominance, personal advancement, work-life balance. The list is very long. In some cases, these agendas contribute to the success of the organization. In other cases, they may take away from it. Some modified version of "my way or the highway" can become necessary. My sense is that some employees may resist that approach, but others may welcome it as a way of reducing the kind of chaos and goal uncertainty that can emerge in a large organization.

At a broader level, leaders have to set and stick with a strategic agenda that others may question. An organization may need to make a tough strategic decision—for example, reducing costs in difficult circumstances or making a bet-the-farm investment. How does a complex organization decide to do that? In most cases, this sort of decision comes from the CEO. There may be a lot of discussion and a lot of different opinions before and after such a decision, but a leader cut from the cloth of Staley or Hurley is not going to be pushed off that agenda.

Does a Lack of Overt Intensity Mean a Lack of Desire?

Having pointed out some qualities of intensity that I believe can transfer to the corporate environment, it's important to note that some CEOs who play to win every day do not feel it's necessary to demonstrate a Staley/Hurley level of intensity and don't find it natural to behave that way. Tim Cook at Apple is probably the number one example. Apple plays to win. Look at its results over all these years, the extraordinary profitability, incredible capitalization in the publicly traded markets, continued strong product after strong product, and dominant market position. Yet nobody would ever accuse Tim Cook of being Dan Hurley or Dawn Staley.

Some organizational cultures simply will not tolerate a take-no-prisoners leadership personality. However, in some sports teams, and probably some corporate organizations, that personality will be tolerated, but only while the team, or company, is winning. As soon as they stop winning, the powers that be may decide that the results are no longer sufficient to tolerate a highly intense temperament in the leader.

The Necessity of Intensity

I would invite anyone reading this blog, anyone with a strong interest in leadership, to look hard at Dawn Staley and Dan Hurley—at the grit of their backgrounds, the intensity of their styles, and the unquestionably successful results they have achieved. Although some characteristics of their intensity are probably simply not feasible in a complex organizational environment, I believe we all need to ask ourselves whether truly important results can be achieved without a level of intensity that would be considered out of the ordinary.

Let's be honest. Bringing the intensity of the Staleys and Hurleys of the world into a traditional business environment would likely burn out traditional corporate executives, not to mention their entire organizations. However, that is not to say that there isn't something important to take away from leaders in the sports or corporate worlds who may appear to function at a hotter temperature than most.

In a lot of organizations today, that level of intensity is pretty much unacceptable from the get-go—that kind of single-mindedness, achievement-orientation, desire to not just be good, but to be the best. Yet, the highest level of achievement absolutely requires some kind of over-the-top intensity. It might not be manifested in the way that Hurley and Staley manifest it. But in our most successful leaders—in the goals and objectives they're trying to achieve, and in the way they function in the managerial and business environment—the essence of Staley and Hurley burns bright.

References

[1] Raynor, G.: "Dawn Staley 'is Philadelphia': Stories from the City That Loves Her Back." *The Athletic*, Apr 7, 2024.

[2] Smith, B.: "UConn Head Coach Dan Hurley, 'The Competitor.'" *Sports Illustrated*, Mar. 27, 2023.

[3] Wolken, D. "UConn's Dan Hurley is the Perfect Sports Heel. So Kentucky Job Would be a Perfect Fit." *USA Today*, Apr. 9, 2024.

Don't Let Your Hospital Be Boeing

FEBRUARY 14, 2024

With Allan Frankel, MD, Executive Principal, Vizient

I f you haven't noticed (but I am sure you have) American business can be very unsettling from time to time, and occasionally the bigger the business, the more unsettling it gets. Exhibit A right now for this observation is, of course, the Boeing Company.

For years Boeing was an iconic, high reliability company—a worldwide leader in the growth of airplane transportation. As Bill Saporito wrote in the January 23 *New York Times*, Boeings' airplanes were industry-changing, including the 707 jet in 1957, the 747 introduced in 1970, and perhaps the most successful commercial plane in aviation history, the 737.[1]

But when things go bad, they can, indeed, go very bad. The newly designed 737 MAX crashed twice, once in 2018 and again in 2019, with a loss of life of 346 people. Now this year, a door plug fell off the Alaska Airlines Boeing 737 Max 9 at 16,000 feet and subsequent investigation revealed the possibility of missing bolts. All 737 MAX 9s were grounded while a special investigation was convened. Manufacturing airplanes is a special enterprise; lives are at stake. Airlines and the flying public take these Boeing problems very seriously.

What went wrong at Boeing? Everybody has an opinion. One popular interpretation goes all the way back to Boeing's merger in 1997 with McDonell Douglas. Recent articles suggest that prior to

1997 Boeing had a very dominant "engineering" culture. After the McDonell Douglas merger, the Boeing culture took a more "business" turn. That is the speculation anyway. What strikes me here is the similarity between Boeing and the American hospital industry. Boeing "manufactures" planes and hospitals "manufacture" healthcare. Neither industry can make mistakes; manufacturing errors in both cases change lives and cause real personal and societal pain. For both Boeing and hospitals, high reliability and error-free execution is the only acceptable business model.

Why is this analogy to Boeing apt and important? Because American healthcare is likely the most intricate enterprise humanity has ever engineered. Therapeutic interventions are increasingly effective but demand pinpoint diagnoses and precision treatment. All of this is happening within profound technological complexity. The opportunity for regrettable manufacturing error—in fact the likelihood of such error—is so significant that no American hospital can possibly take for granted that high reliability processes and culture are properly in place and remain in place.

So what can hospitals do to keep from being Boeing? In all candor, this question is over my paygrade, so for an experienced and nuanced answer, I turned to Allan Frankel, MD. Dr. Frankel is an anesthesiologist and former hospital executive who founded Safe and Reliable Healthcare after evaluating one too many disasters in healthcare delivery. He is currently an Executive Principal at Vizient Inc. Dr. Frankel offered the following high reliability tutorial:

1. High reliability manufacturing is directly dependent on the culture of the organization in question. Everyday excellence which leads to high reliability is dependent on the collective mindset and social norms of your workforce. Any high reliability workforce must trust its leadership and believe that the workforce values and leadership values are aligned. Further, a high reliability

culture gives the workforce a sense of purpose and the opportunity to be their best professional selves on the job.

2. In the workplace, bi-directional communication is essential. Leaders and managers must round, see the actual work first-hand, learn what it is like to perform the work, and talk to individuals about the challenges of doing the work. Under best practices senior leaders should round 10% to 20% of their time. Line managers should round 80% to 90% of their time.

3. Workers, on the other hand, must have a sense of voice and agency. Voice means that workers are able to speak up about their concerns and ideas. Agency means that when workers do speak up, they see their ideas and concerns influence their work environment for the better.

4. Voice and agency require that workers feel safe in the high reliability process and that when identifying defects in the manufacturing process, they will be treated fairly. And importantly, that having the courage to speak up is an organizational attribute that is perceived as worthy. Such worthiness is described by discrete concepts including "psychological safety," just culture," and "respect." Each of these concepts is definable and requires focused and ongoing training.

5. Concepts 3 and 4 require close attention and care and feeding. Functionally, this happens by robust leader rounding, robust managerial huddles, and timely feedback regarding manufacturing concerns and weaknesses. These activities need to be structural and must be built into a system of operations—such systems are often referred to as "standard work." These changes plus the right frame of mind functionally drive improvement and change. Dr. Frankel noted "it's not complicated, but as the Boeing example illustrates, the high reliability philosophy must be perpetually nourished."

6. Once all the above is in place, there needs to be an effector arm. Process improvement skills are required to take ideas and concerns and test and implement them. Quality personnel must check on the changes as they are being made and audit operations. Dr. Frankel adds that this part of the high reliability journey is very often under-resourced in healthcare organizations, with the result that the overall process feels less effective so the activities stop occurring.

7. Training and skills are paramount. Skills come from training and reading. You should be thinking here about the "10,000 hours concept."[2] Worthy attitudes must be defined by your organization and then uniformly expected of all staff. Finally, behaviors can be structured, expectations set, and measures and metrics identified.

As you can see from the suggested activities, the foundations of high reliability are not rocket science. They require the right frame of mind, attention to detail, and clear accountability of all involved. No hospital should let that metaphorical 737 MAX 9 door plug fall off at 16,000 feet. It was, without question, a terrifying manufacturing moment.

References

1 Saporito, B.: "Boeing Made a Change to Its Corporate Culture Decades Ago. Now It's Paying the Price." *The New York Times*, Jan. 23, 2024.

2 Wong, N.C.: "The 10,000-Hour Concept." *Canadian Urological Association Journal*, Sept.-Oct. 2015.

The Leadership Theories of Coach John Wooden: "Be Quick—But Don't Hurry"

JANUARY 31, 2024

The struggle continues as hospital executives work overtime to return their organizations to necessary profitability, essential competitiveness, and offering an appropriate level of clinical access. As noted in this blog several months ago, management guru Peter Drucker always maintained that hospitals were the hardest of all American organizations to run successfully.[1] If Drucker were still alive, he would—without question—double down on that observation.

The question must be asked whether historical hospital leadership structures and strategies are still adequate to cope with a fast-changing healthcare industry that features a different level of financial problems, an unrecognizable workforce, and a shape-shifting patient population? This is a leadership question that requires a thoughtful and sophisticated answer. To paraphrase Albert Einstein, we cannot solve our hospital management problems with the same level of leadership that created them.

So, we are collectively on the hunt for leadership and managerial solutions. The leadership ideas must be different, original, and challenge conventional thinking. Successful healthcare executives these days must be active readers and learners. Winning ideas are everywhere but you need to be both curious and aggressive to find them.

In that regard, let's turn our curiosity toward the theories and teachings of Coach John Wooden. For our younger readers, John Wooden was the coach of the of the UCLA men's basketball program from 1948 to 1975. During that time, he won 10 NCAA national championships in 12 years and at one point his teams won 88 games in a row. ESPN's "Page 2" readers voted him the greatest coach of all time.[2] But John Wooden wasn't just a basketball coach; he was a manager, an executive, a teacher, and a philosopher. There was nothing random or laissez-faire about his approach to leadership. Coach Wooden led through a series of principles that he applied with absolute consistency. Players changed, the opposition changed, and external factors changed, but Coach Wooden's essential approach to leadership did not vary or change.

The central tenet of Coach Wooden's leadership philosophy was the somewhat Zen-like principle of "be quick—but don't hurry." At first blush, this organizing principle doesn't seem to make much sense, especially to the casual reader. John Wooden believed and taught that there were two keys to successful performance, both in sports and otherwise. First, quickness and a sense of urgency was absolutely necessary to winning in a competitive environment. But for Coach Wooden, quickness itself was not sufficient for consistent success. Quickness had to be accompanied by emotional and professional balance in order to achieve team and organizational excellence. So, from Coach Wooden's perspective, a great athlete or a great executive had to not just move and think quickly, but also had to make sure that he or she was moving to a place of personal balance. Coach Wooden believed that this concept of personal balance was the key to real success at both the team and individual level. To find that place of balance you needed to be quick, but to retain that balance you had to be sure not to hurry. In other words, "be quick—but don't hurry."

"Be quick—but don't hurry" was the central principle of John Wooden's leadership style but "be quick—but don't hurry" was also the platform on which an entire management and leadership theory was built. This led to other key Wooden tenets including:

Focus on effort, not winning. Amazingly for a coach that won 10 national championships, the UCLA players always said that Coach Wooden never talked much about winning. Instead, he talked about individual and team effort. He talked about the process, the belief that the right leadership combined with exceptional effort would inevitably deliver remarkable results.

A good leader is first a teacher. John Wooden's first job out of college was teaching high school English. And for the rest of his career, he always thought of himself as a teacher. Wooden taught through four components: demonstration, imitation, correction, and repetition. Coach Wooden had this absolutely right from my perspective: To be a great leader and executive, you almost always have to be a great teacher first.

Teamwork is a necessity. Bill Walton, one of Coach Wooden's most accomplished and greatest players, said it best: "Coach Wooden challenged us to believe that something special could come from the group effort. We live in a society that is constantly pushing us to be individual, to be selfish. But Coach Wooden constantly focused on the group, and how there could be no success unless everybody believed in the same goal and everybody came out of there feeling good about the success of others."

Failing to prepare is preparing to fail. This quote is often attributed to Coach Wooden, but it was first said by Benjamin Franklin.[3] Coach Wooden was extraordinarily well-prepared. Even after years and years of amazing and unprecedented success, Coach

Wooden still scripted each and every practice. He was famous for arriving to practice early to make sure everything was in order and that, in fact, he and the team were completely prepared to get the most out of that afternoon. Hospitals and health systems have "practices" as well: They are called "meetings." What is the standard for preparation in your hospital organization? What is the quality of the work both before and after meetings? What is the level of preparation for consequential meetings such as rating agency presentations, Board approval of major initiatives, and important discussions with external parties? The longer my consulting and business career goes on, the more I have come to believe in and rely on impeccable preparation.

This blog covers just a few of Coach Wooden's many approaches to and commentaries on management and leadership. But the above observations are a useful start. It is important to disclose that this blog post was guided by and drew quotes from an excellent book, *Be Quick—But Don't Hurry: Finding Success in the Teachings of a Lifetime*,[4] which was written by Andrew Hill (a former UCLA player) with the assistance of John Wooden. The book was published by Simon & Schuster in 2001 but as readers can easily see, the book by Messrs. Hill and Wooden remains absolutely relevant today. The book is a short read but will prove to be a good use of your time and your curiosity.

Learn and be smart. Those are the key attributes for today's healthcare executives. Yesterday's executive techniques are no longer getting the job done. Hospital leaders must be better in order to deal with the long list of obstacles that are preventing hospital success. Coach Wooden invented a unique roadmap to executive learning and leadership. That Wooden roadmap is definitely "old school," but that roadmap and its attendant theories and methods are absolutely worth your attention.

References

1   Kaufman, K., Swanson, E.: "Management of Labor in Trying Financial Circumstances." Kaufman Hall, Jul. 28, 2023.

2   Greene, J.: "Page 2 Readers Vote Wooden Top Coach." ESPN, Jun. 10, 2010.

3   "Thoughts on the Business of Life," *Forbes*.

4   Hill, A., Wooden, J.: *Be Quick—But Don't Hurry: Finding Success in the Teachings of a Lifetime.* Simon & Schuster, 2001.

The Emotional IQ of Leadership

JANUARY 10, 2024

I recently had dinner with my good friend and colleague, Dave Blom. For many years, Dave was the President and CEO of Ohio Health. During his tenure, Ohio Health was one of America's most successful health systems by any measure. Dave Blom was known nationally as a calm, steady, and thoughtful hospital leader.

Dave and I were talking about the difficulties of leading and managing complex healthcare organizations in the post-COVID era. The hospital problems of finance, staffing, access, and inflation have been well itemized and documented. While the day-to-day operating problems are undeniably significant and persistent, Dave and I agreed that the hospital leadership issues that really matter right now center around the ability of hospital executives to possess and demonstrate an authentic emotional IQ to lead a diverse workforce in such difficult circumstances.

Such a realization is supported by the recognition that no matter how technically excellent they are, hospitals are just not like other organizations in other industries. Taking care of patients—in fact, taking care of communities—is not only managerially complicated but emotionally testing. Leadership gets much more complicated in the current environment.

Having moved the conversation to this point Dave and I then took on the definition of a workable and effective leadership emotional IQ. That emotional IQ is characterized by the following:

Empathy. During COVID, when leadership was challenged at every level and at every American organization, the value of personal empathy moved to the forefront. Empathy is defined as "the ability to understand and share the feelings of another." More directly, a hospital CEO needs to understand and share the feelings of his or her entire organization. Great hospital leaders understand the difference between sympathy and empathy. Sympathy is a passive emotion, an emotion that notes and cares about a problem but doesn't necessarily act on that problem. Empathy is an active emotion. A leader with empathy not only notes the problem but immediately moves to be of help either at the personal or organizational level, whichever is required.

Vulnerability. Vulnerability is defined as "the willingness to show emotion or to allow one's weakness to be seen or known." Historically, executive leadership—especially in corporate situations—has been trained and encouraged not to show emotion or weakness. But organizations are changing, and the composition of the hospital workforce is different. The patient care process is emotional in and of itself and the daily operational interaction demands a different kind of leadership—a leadership that is comfortable with both emotion and weakness.

Humility. Executives who show humility "are willing to ask for help and don't insist on everything done their way; they are quick to forgive and are known for their patience." Humility also reflects changing organizational ecosystems. Humility is not generally indicative or compatible with the "military command" model of leadership. It is more supportive of a collaborative and cooperative leadership model, which has at its core a heavy dose of decentralization and delegation.

As our dinner was coming to a close, we took note of two other leadership observations. First, when you create a leadership team that fully embraces the principles of empathy, vulnerability, and humility, then that emotional IQ combination creates the highest order goal of organizational trust. All of this is exceptionally meaningful since organizational trust is more important than ever, given that it is in such short supply at all levels of American society. Dave Blom then advanced the discussion to one further point. When you gain the full value of empathy, vulnerability, and humility and you add to that the organizational trust you have established, all the principled prerequisites for establishing corporate and managerial integrity are in place. Empathy plus vulnerability plus humility equals organizational trust. And then empathy plus vulnerability plus humility plus trust equals organizational integrity.

The emotional IQ of leadership is not created by accident. It requires a hyper-aware organization at both the management and Board level. It requires governance and executive leaders who understand that hospital success cannot be achieved by technical and clinical excellence alone. That success must be built on a platform of an emotional IQ that is supported, valued, and shared by the entire hospital community.

Executive Intelligence and Its Relationship to Management Competence

DECEMBER 13, 2023

These days I have been reading *From Strength to Strength: Finding Success, Happiness, and Deep Purpose in the Second Half of Life* by Arthur C. Brooks.[1] Brooks is the former President of the American Enterprise Institute and is currently a professor at both the Harvard Kennedy School and the Harvard Business School. *From Strength to Strength* is a book about intelligence and aging and the relationship of those aspects to personal happiness. The book is part sociology, part psychology, and part self-help. But if you read carefully, the book also offers important lessons in contemporary management.

The central theme of *From Strength to Strength* is how our intelligence changes over time and how individuals must change to make the best use of this changing intelligence. To make this point, Brooks cites Raymond Cattell, a British-American psychologist, who in 1971 suggested that there are two types of intelligence: "fluid intelligence" and "crystallized intelligence."[2] Cattell and Brooks define fluid intelligence as the ability to "reason, think flexibly, and solve novel problems." This is the kind of smarts and intelligence that is associated with young Nobel Prize winners and the tech titans of Silicon Valley. Crystallized intelligence is different. Brooks defines crystallized intelligence as the ability to use a stock of knowledge accumulated and learned in the past. Fluid intelligence is a characteristic of the young while crystallized intelligence is more closely associated with our aging process. At its best, fluid intelligence is "raw smarts" or what I might term "mental athleticism." Crystallized intelligence at its best is what we recognize as "wisdom."

Extrapolating from Brooks' observations and analysis, one can conclude that complex organizations, both not-for-profit and for-profit, require both kinds of executive intelligence. Fluid intelligence generates new ideas, top-shelf innovation, and executive solutions to the most difficult business problems. But crystallized intelligence provides organizations with "the wisdom and experience of people who have seen a lot." To further paraphrase Brooks, crystallized intelligence can teach the organization how not to make flagrant, self-defeating, and avoidable errors.

Reading Brooks and thinking about Cattell's research led me to two observations. First, in our general corporate environment, including hospitals, we very much de-emphasize the value of crystallized intelligence. Just at the moment when many "older" executives are at the highest point of institutional wisdom, our modern corporate structure tends to react in two ways:

- In general, we no longer give these so-called older executives jobs of responsibility and/or importance. These jobs are reserved for younger executives whose critical qualification is powerful levels of fluid intelligence.

- Also, many corporate organizations demand what I would characterize as "early retirement." This is especially true in many prominent American companies when long-tenured executives are required to retire in their late fifties or early sixties. If you place these retirements in the context of crystallized intelligence, then such retirements inevitably lead to a significant loss of human capital to our overall national economy. This includes the loss of long-term accumulated smarts, and most importantly, a loss of organizational wisdom.

Turning this discussion more specifically to hospital management leads to my second observation. Since COVID, the number of hospital CEO resignations has significantly increased when compared to previous years. Additionally, not only has CEO turnover increased but a number of important, influential, and highly capable CEOs—who previously might have been expected to work into their mid-sixties or, perhaps, even into their early seventies—have also decided to leave hospital leadership.

If we come back then to the central observations of Brooks and Cattell, we can see that hospital leadership and management, which is already challenged by so many external and difficult factors, is now losing critically required crystallized intelligence and wisdom.

Having said all this, it is still patently obvious that your organization requires the fluid intelligence of the next generation and the generation after that. That kind of intelligence is necessary and essential to solve today's and tomorrow's hardest healthcare problems. And, of course, to innovate and then to innovate some more.

But at the same time, your hospital or health system must also preserve a prominent place for older executives who possess the crystallized intelligence that assures your hospital will prioritize caring, thoughtfulness, and an essential level of managerial balance—all things that come along with executive wisdom.

From Strength to Strength signals a new way of looking at your executive team. This includes understanding that executives of differing tenures bring very different types of intelligence to the organization. And, it requires finding the proper balance between fluid and crystallized intelligence to give your hospital the very best opportunity to re-find its way to a much-needed new vision of hospital success.

References

1   Brooks, A.C.: *From Strength to Strength: Finding Success, Happiness, and Deep Purpose in the Second Half of Life*. Penguin Random House, 2022.
2   "Raymond Cattell." Harvard University Department of Psychology website.

Listening and Learning

OCTOBER 4, 2023

S omething I have been writing about and speaking about recently is how difficult it is to operate a hospital in post-COVID America. The line-up of management and governing obstacles includes both old and new healthcare issues:

- Financial instability
- Ongoing labor disruption
- Remnants of significant healthcare inflation
- Payer chaos
- A continuing pivot from inpatient to outpatient services
- The endless introduction of alternative care options (CVS, Walgreens, Walmart, Amazon, and now Costco)

It takes considerable hard thinking within executive suites to figure out the best way forward; to find the best roadmap through—at a minimum—the six obstacles outlined above. And as I have noted in my recent speaking engagements, a solution to one of these obstacles might actually make others of these obstacles more difficult to solve.

I have in recent weeks been looking for a "thought platform" that can assist hospital C-suite executives in resetting managerial expectations and operational initiatives—expectations and initiatives that can more effectively cope with the current and distressingly difficult environment.

Moving the hospital organizational thought platform from its 2019 managerial themes to a more relevant platform that better suits the challenges of 2023 is a managerial problem all of its own. Simply telling a large and very complex healthcare organization to stop thinking in pre-COVID terms is not likely to accomplish much. Before you can establish the organizational thought platform that best guides your hospital forward, you will need a leadership team that is committed to creating a "listening and learning" healthcare company.

A good tool for making your way to a listening and learning organization and eventually to a new and more relevant thought platform is the book *The First 90 Days: Proven Strategies for Getting Up to Speed Faster and Smarter* by Michael D. Watkins.[1] Mr. Watkins is a co-founder of Genesis Advisers and a professor at the IMD Business School in Lausanne, Switzerland. *The First 90 Days* was originally published in 2003 as a guide to business executives moving into new senior positions of major responsibility. But the book also contains general management advice which is relevant not only to new jobs, but also to executives struggling with fast-changing and especially difficult market conditions. One of the most compelling chapters in *The First 90 Days* is a chapter that focuses on the absolute importance of executive learning and the need to accelerate that learning. While Professor Watkins was making a general business point, I would suggest that the need to accelerate executive learning and listening was never more important than in the "right now" post-COVID healthcare environment. Professor Watkins posed a series of critical leadership learning questions that I have modified to reflect the complex operating conditions of the 2023 hospital. From that perspective, here are six critical learning questions for the hospital leadership team:

1. How effective are you as a hospital leader at learning about your current job and how that current job is changing?

2. What is your learning agenda for your current assignment? Have your day-to-day responsibilities changed so dramatically that you no longer know what you need to know?

3. Given questions one and two, how should you go about gaining better insight?

4. What is the best structure for being a top-flight learner within your organization? Note that this is a question that has both individual and organizational implications.

5. What support is there within your organization for ongoing day-to-day learning? Note this should not be viewed as "training." This is how executives "learn" through constant interaction with their changing jobs and changing market conditions. We are headed here not toward "skillsets" but toward "learned strategies and insights." The difference is material.

6. Professor Watkins suggests creating a learning agenda that relates directly to an ongoing learning plan. What don't you know right now and how are you going to learn what you don't know? And, importantly, how has the healthcare macroeconomy made your job more difficult and why?

One of my last blogs[2] focused on the importance of vision and strategy in the post-COVID hospital recovery process; the importance of reinventing the hospital of the future that best fits into a rapidly changing marketplace. This marketplace requires entirely new skillsets and functions on top of changing shared experiences and perceived social values. Finding the right going-forward strategy and vision is the first imperative. But without executive learning and listening that leads directly to organizational-wide learning and listening, the chances of finding your way to that highest and best and most effective vision and strategy will be greatly diminished.

References

[1] Watkins, M.D.: *The First 90 Days: Proven Strategies for Getting Up to Speed Faster and Smarter*. Harvard Business Review Press, 2013.

[2] Kaufman, K.: "'Culture Eats Strategy for Breakfast' But Probably Not Right Now." Kaufman Hall, Aug. 30, 2023.

Lessons from the Final Four

APRIL 1, 2022

The regular season of the men's Division 1 NCAA college basketball season began on November 9, 2021, and concluded on March 13, 2022, In that time, 358 teams played more than 5,000 games.

As of March 30, the date I am writing this blog, 68 teams played 64 games in the NCAA Championship Tournament.

At this point in that long and competitive regular-season and post-season journey, we are left with four teams standing: Duke, Kansas, North Carolina, and Villanova.

If the teams in this year's Final Four look familiar, there is a reason. Since the NCAA men's basketball tournament began in 1939, Duke, Kansas, North Carolina, and Villanova have participated in a combined 58 Final Fours. Between them, they have won 17 national championships.

To reach the Final Four in any single NCAA season is a major achievement. And this level of success, over many years against formidable competition, is no accident. It is the result of elements that only a few university men's basketball programs have been able to fully achieve and sustain over time. And the elements that these blue-blood basketball programs have are the elements of success for any enterprise, particularly in today's economy.

Management (coaching) excellence. Coach K, Bill Self, Hubert Davis, and Jay Wright are extraordinary leaders. They combine deep knowledge, strategic insight, organizational savvy, relentless drive, and superb motivational skills. There is no substitute for extraordinary leadership.

Resources and facilities. These schools make it a point to invest extravagantly in their basketball programs. All four are in the top 20 of university basketball program spending, and Duke is number 1. This level of investment gives their programs significant advantages in areas such as coaching, recruiting, and training.

A tradition of excellence. Winning is an ethic and a culture. An enterprise that succeeds year-in and year-out expects to win. These organizations know the resources, execution, and drive that go into winning, and they know how to marshal them every day and every year. They go into every situation with confidence, and with the fundamentals and history to back up that confidence.

The sustained experience of success. Top-flight enterprises are successful because they are successful. Success brings additional financial resources. Additional financial resources bring better tools and talent. It is no surprise that opportunity knocks repeatedly at the address of successful enterprises; the best people and the best organizations want to be part of that success.

The expectation of success. Organizations that win don't expect to fail or perform poorly. Winning against all comers is the expectation. These organizations hate to lose, and the occasional inevitable losses are routinely transformed into fuel for future success.

In any tournament, we have upsets. Inevitably, an underdog makes a serious run at the title, such as we had this year when Saint Peter's became the first 15-seed to reach the Elite Eight, and in the process wreaked havoc on my bracket. This phenomenon is inevitable. Statistics 101 tells us that any single head-to-head match-up carries the significant probability of the underdog winning.

However, true enterprise success is never an upset. It is not a one-time occurrence against the odds, but rather a set of attributes that successful organizations put forth over the years.

In today's economy, scale, aggressiveness, and ambition are central to success. Success over time has helped certain dominant companies grow to huge scale, and that level of scale is a platform for sustained success because of their advantageous access to financial and intellectual resources.

These companies are also successful because they have had the most imaginative, aggressive, and motivational leaders—some of the greatest business leaders of our time or any time.

And these companies are successful because winning is part of their culture. They pursue with the intention of dominating entire industry verticals and transforming how people interact with technology. And when failures occur, whether it's a disappointing product launch or a bad earnings quarter, these organizations don't back down, they double down.

The long-term attributes of this year's Final Four are certainly the attributes of success in college basketball. They are also the attributes of success for businesses in a scaled economy. Whatever sort of enterprise you participate in, these observations form your own playbook for success in our current business environment.

What Would You Do If You Were CEO of State Farm?

DECEMBER 12, 2021

The well-worn phrase "culture eats strategy for breakfast" has new relevance in American business these days.

Take the case of State Farm insurance. For almost ten years, Green Bay quarterback Aaron Rodgers has been a spokesperson for the company. Rodgers' 13 years as starting quarterback with the Green Bay Packers and man-of-the-people persona seemed an excellent fit for State Farm, whose friendly "like a good neighbor" slogan has defined the 94-year-old Bloomington, Illinois-based company since 1971.

And all was well. That is, all was well until November 3, 2021, when the Green Bay Packers announced that Rodgers had tested positive for COVID-19.[1] Several days later, Rodgers revealed that he was not vaccinated,[2] contrary to his previous statement that "I've been immunized." Rodgers said that he "found a long term immunization protocol to protect myself, and I'm very proud of the research that went into that." That protocol included ivermectin, a drug whose only FDA-approved use in tablet form for humans is to treat conditions caused by parasitic worms.[3]

Rodgers presented himself as a victim of contemporary culture, saying, "I realize I'm in the crosshairs of the woke mob right now." Rodgers continued, "I'm somebody who's a critical thinker. I march to the beat of my own drum. I believe strongly in bodily autonomy."[4]

The response was swift and decisive, including belittling headlines (like the *Washington Post* opinion piece "When did Dr. Aaron Rodgers, QB, acquire a PhD in epidemiology?"[5]), rebuttal from the NFL of Rodgers' statements about the league's COVID-19 protocols,[6] and seemingly endless mocking on Twitter.[7]

But Rodgers also received support. Former NHL player (and singer Carrie Underwood's husband) Mike Fisher posted to his 578,000 followers on Instagram, "I stand with Aaron Rodgers.... I believe in the freedom to choose what we put in our bodies and the freedom of conscience."[8] Sports talk radio has been divided between those who agree and disagree with Rodgers' stance on vaccination.[9]

Indeed, the public remains sharply divided on COVID vaccination, and that divide is especially sharp between political parties. The Kaiser Family Foundation COVID-19 Vaccine Monitor Dashboard shows that 31% of Republicans say they will "definitely not" get vaccinated, compared with only 2% of Democrats.[10] And the election results of November 2nd show that the nation continues to be politically polarized.

Equally striking is the gap in how geography affects vaccination beliefs and behavior. Among rural individuals, 33% say they will "definitely not" get vaccinated, compared to only 13% among urban populations and 14% among suburban.[11]

Against that backdrop, let's return to our point of departure: State Farm.

Imagine that you are the CEO of State Farm. Your longtime celebrity spokesperson, featured on many television commercials, has made highly controversial statements. What would you do?

In the past, your path forward as CEO might have been relatively clear. If the celebrity's statements were provably false and getting significant bad publicity, get a new celebrity spokesperson.

Today, however, the cultural circumstances in the nation are very different than they have ever been before. Beliefs have replaced facts as a basis for opinion. With a public whose opinions are supercharged, and starkly divided by political affiliation and geography, dropping your celebrity spokesperson will delight a significant portion of your customers and infuriate a significant portion of your customers.

What would you do? How do you weigh the potential implications for the company's policyholders, potential customers, employees, financial position, competitive position, mission, and values? Which direction would do the least damage to the company? Which could do the most good for the company?

As I pointed out in my last blog, reading America's culture correctly has become a prerequisite to successful Board and management decision making.[12] For healthcare organizations with a charitable mission, that decision-making process is especially subtle. Not only do healthcare executives need to weigh the effects of culture on their organizations' financial and competitive positions, but also their mission and values as stewards of community health.

Have you come up with your decision? If you have, I'll now tell you what State Farm did.

It punted. The company issued a carefully worded statement that said, in part:

"Aaron Rodgers has been a great ambassador for our company for much of the past decade. We don't support some of the statements that he has made, but we respect his right to have his own personal point of view. We recognize our customers, employees, agents and brand ambassadors come from all walks of life, with differing viewpoints on many issues. Our mission at State Farm is to support safer, stronger communities. To that end, we encourage vaccinations, but respect everyone's right to make a choice based on their personal circumstances."[13]

State Farm continued to air commercials with Rodgers, but far fewer than before the controversy.

Aaron Rodgers also is a spokesperson for Prevea Health, a multi-specialty group in 80+ locations across Northern, Eastern, and Western Wisconsin. Or, rather, he *was* a spokesperson. Prevea Health's statement on the Rodgers situation contrasts sharply with State Farm's:

"Prevea Health and Aaron Rodgers have made the decision to end their partnership effective Nov. 6, 2021….Prevea Health remains deeply committed to protecting its patients, staff, providers and communities amidst the COVID-19 pandemic. This includes encouraging and helping all eligible populations to become vaccinated against COVID-19 to prevent the virus from further significantly impacting lives and livelihoods. There will be no additional information or interviews available from Prevea Health regarding this subject."[14]

The question "what would you do?" is far from theoretical. Given the divisive, changing, and intense culture of our nation, and its proven effects on markets, any executive, at any time, could be in a similar situation.

References

1   Shook, N.: "Packers QB Aaron Rodgers Tests Positive for COVID-19, Will Not Play in Week 9 vs. Chiefs." NFL, Nov. 3, 2021.

2   *The Pat McAfee Show*, Nov. 5, 2021.

3   "Ivermectin and COVID-19." U.S. Food & Drug Administration, Apr. 5, 2024.

4   *The Pat McAfee Show*, Nov. 5, 2021.

5   Boot, M.: "When Did Dr. Aaron Rodgers, QB, Acquire a PhD in Epidemiology?" *Washington Post*, Nov. 8, 2021.

6   "NFL Releases Statement Slamming Aaron Rodgers' Vaccine Comments." Today Show (via YouTube), Nov. 7, 2021.

7   Radcliffe, J.R.: "Hoo Boy, There is a Lot of Social Media Reaction Following Aaron Rodgers' Comments on COVID-19 Vaccine." *Milwaukee Journal Sentinel*, Nov. 5, 2021.

8   Fisher, M.: "I Stand With Aaron Rodgers." Instagram post, Nov. 6, 2021.

9   Zimmerman, J.: "Rodgers Controversy Dominates Talk on Local Sports Radio." WBAY, Nov. 5, 2021.

10 *KFF COVID-19 Vaccine Monitor*. Kaiser Family Foundation.

11 *KFF COVID-19 Vaccine Monitor*. Kaiser Family Foundation.

12 Kaufman, K.: "Getting Culture Right." Kaufman Hall, Nov. 10, 2021.

13 Brennan, C.: "State Farm Stands by Aaron Rodgers After His Vaccine Comments: 'Respect His Right' to Have His Own Point of View." *USA Today*, Nov. 8, 2021.

14 "An Announcement from Prevea Health and Aaron Rodgers Regarding Their Partnership." Prevea Health, Jul. 8, 2022.

Getting Culture Right

NOVEMBER 10, 2021

Today, American culture is changing so quickly and with such a high degree of nuance that it is increasingly difficult both to interpret and to navigate. However, navigating how those changes affect markets is essential for business success throughout the economy.

For business executives, viewing their markets through the lens of culture can bring the rewards of increased sales, revenue, and consumer loyalty. In contrast, especially with social media that amplifies voices of discontent to ear-splitting levels, companies that miss cultural cues on their markets can find themselves with lost market share, declining revenue, and even public embarrassment.

One of the most notable cultural misses in American business was Victoria's Secret. For decades, the Victoria's Secret brand was represented by rail-thin, airbrushed images of women. As body inclusivity gained traction in the past decade, Victoria's Secret stuck with its outdated depictions, experiencing public backlash, a market share drop from 32% in 2015 to 21% in 2020,[1] and the emergence of new competitors with far more cultural sensitivity.[2] The company's current CEO now acknowledges, "When the world was changing, we were too slow to respond."[3]

At its core, the Victoria's Secret problem was not listening and responding to the cultural changes expressed by its customers. "We needed to stop being about what men want and to be about what women want," its CEO now admits.

In contrast, Old Navy is making contemporary culture core to changes in its business practices. The company spent the past two years listening to its customers, particularly its women customers, and in an open letter "to women everywhere" declared, "It's time to do the thing we always needed to do and completely revolutionize the shopping experience."[4]

Old Navy found that women were highly dissatisfied with the availability of sizes at the company's stores. In-store inventory was oriented toward a limited range of sizes that reflected a societal ideal that shifted from deeply entrenched to outrageously outmoded in a matter of a few years. Larger sizes for women were hard to come by in Old Navy stores, forcing customers who wanted those sizes to shop online in special categories.

Old Navy has pledged that every store will offer all women's styles in sizes 0-28.[5] All sizes will be displayed together, with no special sections for larger sizes. Mannequins will be in sizes four, 12, and 18. On the Old Navy web site, all sizes will be integrated. The company also redesigned its clothing's fit and size standards to be more comfortable and inclusive for all body types.

The company heralded these changes in an advertising campaign featuring highly diverse groups of women and a TV spot featuring Saturday Night Live star Aidy Bryant, all under the banner of what Old Navy calls "BODEQUALITY."

Like Old Navy, America's healthcare organizations must pay attention to the influence of changing culture on their markets and make sure their response is right. Patients and consumers cannot be viewed as a compliant monolith, all going where their health system tells them and all with roughly the same preferences, proclivities, and criteria for satisfaction. COVID has greatly accelerated consumers' experience with new forms of provider engagement, from video visits to care via text to behavioral health apps, and with new providers.

Traditional healthcare organizations need to convey a sense of novelty and currency. They need to offer services borne of cultural consciousness. They need to understand their consumers in a very specific way, from women executives to uninsured gig-economy workers, and design services that embrace the lifestyles and cultural convictions of these audiences. They need to address consumers with words and images that reflect each segment's cultural values.

This overwhelming wave of cultural change is infiltrating every facet of society. I pride myself on keeping up with the latest in business, technology, social movements, music, and art, but I suddenly find myself seeing TV ads for TikTok that are utterly unintelligible to me. This wave of change is affecting the markets that businesses, including healthcare organizations, seek to serve. Some organizations are hyper-sensitive to these changes. Others appear not to see the changes, or perhaps they see but don't understand them, the way I don't understand those TikTok ads.

Old Navy provides an excellent example of a legacy company understanding the cultural changes that are going on in the country and then adjusting its business approach in a major, highly visible way to match that understanding.

Consumers (including patients) will not stay with a company that no longer represents their cultural positions and orientation, and they may even speak out against that company. Any business that gets culture wrong faces the potential consequences of lost loyalty, volume, and revenue. The stakes are especially high for a business as deeply personal as healthcare.

Culture's influence on markets has become especially intense. Reading America's culture correctly has become a prerequisite to successful Board and management decision making. Business is a complicated puzzle, and getting it all right in 2021 is every organization's hardest problem.

References

1 Maheshwari, S., Friedman, V.: "Victoria's Secret Swaps Angels for 'What Women Want.' Will They Buy it?" *The New York Times*, Jun. 16, 2021.

2 Hensel, A.: "As Victoria's Secret's Star Wanes, the Lingerie Market is Growing More Fragmented." *Modern Retail*, Feb. 25, 2020.

3 Maheshwari, S., Friedman, V.: "Victoria's Secret Swaps Angels for 'What Women Want.' Will They Buy it?" *The New York Times*, Jun. 16, 2021

4 "Old Navy Democratizes the Shopping Experience for Women of All Sizes With BODEQUALITY." Gap Inc., Aug. 18, 2021.

5 "Old Navy Democratizes the Shopping Experience for Women of All Sizes With BODEQUALITY." Gap Inc., Aug. 18, 2021.

The Multitasking Enterprise

AUGUST 3, 2020

With Eric Jordahl, Managing Director, Kaufman Hall

For five months, hospital leaders have been responding to what will likely be the biggest challenge of their careers: managing the operational and financial threats from the COVID-19 pandemic. An already difficult environment is likely to become even more challenging this fall and into 2021. Surges and resurges of infection, ongoing macroeconomic threats, and widespread uncertainty about the stability of regained volumes and revenue are likely to persist for some time to come.

Against this backdrop, achieving credit and rating "success" will require significant performance improvement. Given revenue uncertainty and potential volatility, the focus must be on expense containment and careful capital and resource allocation. More than ever before, this will emerge as a rating differentiator.

Preparing for these realities starts with critically assessing every aspect of an organization's toolkit—from financial resources to decision-support infrastructure to management capabilities. This preparation itself will yield clarity, which can be used to guide a more proactive and productive next conversation with rating agencies, investors, and other external constituents. The difference in outcomes from doing this well or doing this poorly will be material.

The ability of executive teams to successfully multitask will be a core driver of success. In this context, multitasking refers to the ability to both confront the myriad of new pressures COVID-19 is producing right now and reposition the risk profile of the organization to be prepared for what is coming next. Organizations have no choice but to address these two priorities simultaneously. And their success will heavily influence whether they thrive or struggle in a post-COVID-19 environment.

Different leaders and organizations possess a wide range of needed multitasking capabilities, which leave them in relatively better or worse position to succeed in the current and emerging environment. As a result, CEOs and hospital boards should be critically assessing right now where their organization finds itself on this key skill continuum, and how to improve its performance.

Enterprise-oriented frameworks that bring analytics and decision-support under a common umbrella are another critical element of improving multitasking. These frameworks—ideally limited to just a few critical needs—can create clarity around resource utilization and risk management, offering senior executives the greatest amount of management leverage. Ultimately, CEOs should be then able to create a "multitasking enterprise," where downstream activities roll up to a manageable and common number of resource deployment and risk management decisions.

As part of this approach, organizations that embrace predictive methodologies can begin to better understand the potential long-term impact of various externalities. At the same time, such methodologies can help identify internal actions to mitigate those external risks. For example, through careful financial planning, organizations might realize the need to move swiftly on securing financing for the next 18 months, or address looming expense problems before they wreak havoc.

In the early days of the COVID-19 pandemic, many disciplined, resilient organizations quickly and simultaneously tackled a wide range of unexpected clinical needs. At the same time, these organizations addressed a rapidly deteriorating financial picture and crafted strategies for the post-COVID-19 world.

As the external environment grows even more uncertain, hospitals will need to take their multitasking to an even more sophisticated, enterprise-wide level. Moving forward, success will require continuous and coordinated monitoring of the external environment, timely evaluation of the associated implications, and proactive steps to mitigate the many, varied, and unpredictable risks of a world that is more volatile than any we have ever experienced.

A Conversation with Jim Collins

JULY 20, 2020

There is not much good that can be said about COVID-19: illness and economic disruption in the extreme, including a major stop to most business travel. The only positive I can think of is that the travel hiatus has opened up more time for quality conversations with clients and colleagues from around the country. A conversation during this period that I greatly valued was with Jim Collins.

In my opinion, Jim Collins is today's most sophisticated thinker about business and leadership issues. I am sure that most of you are familiar with his bestselling books like *Good to Great* and *Great by Choice*. What may not be quite as obvious is that Jim never stops learning and never stops thinking. His research process is intense and rigorous.

Jim and I had a wide-ranging conversation about a variety of leadership issues, but eventually our discussion turned to COVID-19 and the leadership test that the pandemic has presented to healthcare CEOs. The primary question that arose was what would be the personal and organizational characteristics that would separate winners from losers during and after the COVID pandemic.

As we talked, four principles came to the fore that apply to healthcare leaders facing perhaps their greatest professional leadership challenge ever.

Principle One: Readiness

"What organizations do before the storm affects how they perform during the storm"

Organizations that spent their time building the "best house" before the hurricane are most likely to still have the "best house" once the storm passes through. The bulwark of strong healthcare organizations, such as a strong balance sheet, scale, continuous performance improvement, and clinical excellence, are all results of longstanding effort and focus. And the payoff for that longstanding effort is an overall organizational readiness. Ready organizations will weather upheaval in volume, revenue, and the general economic environment. Ready providers pivot quickly to meet new demands. And they take advantage of strategic opportunities that a crisis can bring.

Principle Two: Discipline

"Organizations that are undisciplined when times are good find that such discipline is critical when a crisis hits."

When the pandemic emerged, we saw organizations with the habit of discipline put that habit to work immediately. Inundated with COVID patients, disciplined hospitals set up command-center structures through which daily, or even hourly, reports on issues such as the availability of ICU rooms, ventilators, supplies and workforce were gathered, organized, and acted on.

That same discipline allowed such organizations to multi-task in the midst of clinical chaos. The most disciplined hospitals and systems immediately recognized the need to predict fast-changing financial results, including declines in revenue, profitability, and short-term liquidity, and then to immediately address a cost structure that was no longer properly correlated to declining revenue.

In some cases, all of the above was accomplished in a few short months despite the fact that the clinical demands of COVID were an all-time great managerial distraction.

Principle Three: Competitive Separation

"In times like these, the separation between organizations tends to be permanent, and those that are weaker tend to fall further behind."

Strength translates into strategic flexibility. COVID-19 is very likely to change the overall healthcare competitive dynamic in profound ways. Organizations that went into the pandemic financially challenged will have limited choices coming out of the pandemic. Larger, stronger organizations will build scale and invest in capabilities that will create a better and more permanent competitive position.

As one CEO told us, "If you're going into this strong, use this time to figure out how you advance toward strategies that you could not pursue under normal circumstances."

Principle Four: Durability

"As organizations, we can orient ourselves around transactions or around relationships. Especially during a crisis, the most durable business orientation is around relationships."

Healthcare is a highly transactional undertaking: appointments, exchanges of information, testing and results, billing and receivables—even on occasion diagnoses and treatment. Yet underneath all of these transactions are deeply personal relationships with patients; families; team members; employers; suppliers; local, state, and federal governments; payers; and communities.

During the COVID crisis we heard time and time again about the power of these relationships. Good relationships with vendors and suppliers improved access to PPE and ventilators. Good relationships with local government meant setting aside politics and finding solutions to unprecedented problems. Good relationships with staff fostered a willingness to work in new roles under sometimes harrowing conditions. And good relationships have led to trust as patients return to hospitals for needed care delayed by all things COVID.

Our era of high-tech dominance puts a huge premium on friction-free transactions in everything from grocery shopping to food ordering. And there is no denying the importance of perfectly executed transactions in satisfying consumers and running a world-class hospital.

There is no doubt, however, that COVID-19 has shown again how much high-performing healthcare organizations depend on the goodwill of longstanding relationships at every level of day-to-day operations.

My thanks to Jim Collins for pointing out the deep leadership lessons of recent months. In my opinion Jim is a hall-of-fame thinker and teacher. And he reminds us, once again, that effective leadership begins with the best thinking and teaching that we can all muster.

Issues in Healthcare Strategy and Management

Comments on Current Management Issues in the Healthcare C-Suite: "Culture Eats Strategy for Breakfast" But Probably Not Right Now

AUGUST 3, 2023

With Pete McCanna, Chief Executive Officer, Baylor, Scott & White Health

2022 and 2023 have been particularly difficult operating years for hospital providers. The financial challenges stand out but as we concluded in the August 7, 2023, blog, strategic planning and vision issues may be more compelling over the long term.[1] We previously identified two strategic issues that need to be reckoned with:

1. **Strategic Relevance.** Has everything changed organizationally post-COVID or does it just feel that way? If your strategy still seems dynamic and relevant, how do you capitalize on that? If your strategy feels entirely lost, how do you recapture organizational excitement and enthusiasm?

2. **Vision.** How important is organizational vision right now? You know the old saying, "a camel is a horse designed by a committee." And many vision statements wind up looking more like that camel than like that desired horse. But be that as it may:

COVID has been so disruptive to the organizational momentum of hospitals that finding a relevant and executable vision should be top of mind right now.

Given circumstances, one obvious conclusion is that any strategic exercise undertaken in the current moment needs to be well accomplished. Executive teams, clinicians, and Boards are simply too distracted or too tired to spend time on planning processes that are not well thought out and highly directed. This immediate observation next demands a discussion that outlines post-COVID strategic principles, definitions, and the creation of a vision that relates immediately to actionable strategy. It would be an understatement to note that for hospitals there is no "strategic time" to waste.

Start the post-COVID planning process with four very clear strategic definitions:

1. **Vision:** A time-bounded view of the future destination of your business.
2. **Strategic Workstreams:** The ways you devise to achieve the strategic vision.
3. **Goals:** Goals are the lag outcomes that you seek to achieve for your customers.
4. **Metrics:** Metrics measure the progress toward the goals.

Working from these definitions then allows you to move toward an organizationally appropriate vision and an actionable strategy that efficiently supports that vision as follows:

1. *The vision should drive growth.* Many hospital organizations have stopped growing organically. No growth is harmful financially, clinically, intellectually, and creatively.

2. *The vision should differentiate the business from that of competitors.* Everybody and everything competes with hospitals these days: other hospitals, pharmacy companies, insurers, private equity. It has no end.

3. *The vision should endeavor to solve a basic customer problem or problems.* The problem list is pretty apparent. The list of helpful solutions has been harder to come by.

4. *The vision should be either incremental or transformational.* In all candor, most hospitals' post-COVID vision is going to be incremental. It takes considerable financial and capital capacity to move toward a transformational vision. That kind of capacity is available at only a small minority of hospitals nationwide.

5. *Recognize that a transformational vision will require active management of culture and stakeholders.* If you pivot to a transformational vision, you are likely to upset certain stakeholders and your existing culture may need to also adjust to the transformation.

6. *Be prepared to modify or improve upon the vision, workstreams, and/or goals as you get ongoing feedback during the planning and execution process.* Under any circumstances you need to be open to learning all along the way. For this to happen, your organization needs to be a listening organization and a learning organization. Not all hospitals and health systems are.

Does all this sound hard? It should sound hard because it is hard. Leading the hospital back to financial stability while finding a relevant post-COVID vision that proves to be competitive and, at the same time, energizes your team to find renewed purpose in your hospital's work; that is unforgivably hard. As Piet Hein, the Danish mathematician, profoundly said, "Problems worthy of attack prove their worth by fighting back." And fighting back is the hospital job of the moment.

Note: "Culture eats strategy for breakfast" is a quote attributed to management consultant and writer Peter Drucker.

Reference

1   Kaufman, K.: "Hospital Strategy and Planning in Times of Financial Challenge." Kaufman Hall, Aug. 7, 2023.

The Physician Employment Model, Continued

JULY 14, 2023

From time to time the blogging process stimulates a conversation between the author and the audience. This type of conversation occurred after the publication of my recent blog, "The Hospital Makeover—Part 2." This blog focused entirely on the current problems, financial and otherwise, of the hospital physician employment model. I received responses from CEOs and other C-suite executives and those responses are very much worth adding to the physician employment conversation.

Hospital executives have obviously given the physician employment strategy considerable thought. One CEO noted that, looking back from a business perspective, physician employment was not actually a doctor retention strategy but, in the long run, more of a customer acquisition and customer loyalty strategy. The tactic was to employ the physician and draw his or her patients into the hospital ecosystem. And by extension, if the patient was loyal to the doctor, then the patient would also be loyal to the hospital. Perhaps this approach was once legitimate but new access models, consumerism, and the healthcare preferences of at least two generations of patients have challenged the strategic validity of this tactic. The struggle now—and the financial numbers validate that struggle—is that the physician employment model has become extraordinarily expensive and, from observation, does not scale. Therefore, the relevant business question becomes what are the most efficient and durable customer acquisition and loyalty models now available to hospitals and health systems?

A few more physician employment observations worth sharing:

Primary care. The physician employment model has generally created a one-size-fits all view of primary care. Consumers, however, want choice. They want 32 flavors, not just vanilla. Alternative primary care models need to match up to fast-changing consumer preferences.

Where physician employment works. In general, the employment model has worked where doctor "shift work" is involved. This includes facility-based specialists such as emergency physicians, anesthesiologists, and hospitalists.

Chronic care management. Traditional physician employment models that drive toward doctor-led physical clinics have generally not led to the improved monitoring and treatment of chronic care patient problems. As a result, the chronic care space will likely see significant disruption from virtual and in-home tools.

All in all, the very smart observations detailed above continue the hospital physician employment conversation.

The Hospital Makeover—Part 2

JULY 6, 2023

America's hospitals have a $104 billion problem. That's the amount you arrive at if you multiply the number of physicians employed by hospitals and health systems (approximately 341,200 as of January 2022, according to data from the Physicians Advocacy Institute and Avalere) by the median $306,362 subsidy—or loss—reported in our Q1 2023 *Physician Flash Report.*[1]

Subsidizing physician employment has been around for a long time and such subsidies were historically justified as a loss leader for improved clinical services, the potential for increased market share, and the strengthening of traditionally profitable services. But I am pretty sure the industry did not have $104 billion in losses in mind when the physician employment model first became a key strategic element in the hospital operating model. However, the upward reset in expenses brought on by the pandemic and post-pandemic inflation has made many downstream hospital services that historically operated at a profit now operate at breakeven or even at a loss. The loss leader physician employment model obviously no longer works when it mostly leads to more losses.

This model is clearly broken and in demand of a near-term fix. Perhaps the critical question then is how to begin? How to reconsider physician employment within the hospital operating plan?

Out of the box, rethink the physician productivity model. Our most recent *Physician Flash Report* data shows that for surgical specialties, there was a median $77 net patient revenue per provider wRVU.[2] For the same specialties, there was a median $80 provider paid compensation per provider wRVU. In other words, before any other expenses are factored in, these specialties are losing $3 per wRVU on paid compensation alone. Getting providers to produce more wRVUs only makes the loss bigger. It's the classic business school 101 problem. If a factory is losing $5 on every widget it produces, the answer is not to produce more widgets. Rather, expenses need to come down, whether that is through a readjustment of compensation, new compensation models that reward efficiency, or the more effective use of advanced practice providers.

Second, a number of hospital CEOs have suggested to me that the current employed physician model is quite past its prime. That model was built for a system of care that included generally higher revenues, more inpatient care, and a greater proportion of surgical vs. medical admissions. But overall, these trends were changing and then were accelerated by the COVID pandemic. Inpatient revenue has been flat to down. More clinical work continues to shift to the outpatient setting and, at least for the time being, medical admissions have been more prominent than before the pandemic.

Taking all this into account suggests that in many places the employed physician organizational and operating model is entirely out of balance. One would offer the calculated guess that there are too many coaches on the team and not enough players on the field. This administrative overhead was seemingly justified in a different loss leader environment but now it is a major contributor to that $104 billion industry-wide loss previously calculated.

Finally, perhaps the very idea of physician employment needs to be rethought. My colleagues Matthew Bates and John Andersen have commented that the "owner" model is more appealing to physicians who remain independent then the "renter" model.[3] The current employment model offers physicians stability of practice and income but appears to come at the cost of both a loss of enthusiasm and lost entrepreneurship. The massive losses currently experienced strongly suggest that new models are essential to reclaim physician interest and establish physician incentives that result in lower practice expenses, higher practice revenues, and steadily reduced overall subsidies.

Please see this blog as an extension of my last blog, "America's Hospitals Need a Makeover."[4] It should be obvious that by analogy we are not talking about a coat of paint here or even new appliances in the kitchen. The financial performance of America's hospitals has exposed real structural flaws in the healthcare house. A makeover of this magnitude is going to require a few prerequisites:

1. Don't start designing the renovation unless you know specifically where profitability has changed within your service lines and by explicitly how much. Right now is the time to know how big the problem is, where those problems are located, and what is the total magnitude of the fix.

2. The Board must be brought into the discussion of the nature of the physician employment problem and the depth of its proposed solutions. Physicians are not just "any employees." They are often the engine that runs the hospital and must be afforded a level of communication that is equal to the size of the financial problem. All of this will demand the Board's knowledge and participation as solutions to the physician employment dilemma are proposed, considered, and eventually acted upon.

The basic rule of home renovation applies here as well: the longer the fix to this problem is delayed the harder and more expensive the project becomes. The losses set out here certainly suggest that physician employment is a significant contributing factor to hospitals' current financial problems overall. It would be an understatement to say that the time to get after all of this is right now.

References

[1] Bates, M., Swanson, E.: *Physician Flash Report: Q1 2023*. Kaufman, Hall & Associates, May 3, 2023.

[2] Bates, M., Swanson, E.: *Physician Flash Report: Q1 2023*. Kaufman, Hall & Associates, May 3, 2023.

[3] Bates, M., Andersen, J.: "Renters or Owners: Real Estate and Physician Affiliation." Kaufman Hall, Sept. 23, 2021.

[4] Kaufman, K.: "America's Hospitals Need a Makeover." Kaufman Hall, Jun. 14, 2023.

America's Hospitals
Need a Makeover

JUNE 14, 2023

A couple of months ago, I got a call from a CEO of a regional health system—a long-time client and one of the smartest and most committed executives I know. This health system lost tens of millions of dollars in fiscal year 2022 and the CEO told me that he had come to the conclusion that he could not solve a problem of this magnitude with the usual and traditional solutions. Pushing the pre-COVID managerial buttons was just not getting the job done.

This organization is fiercely independent. It has been very successful in almost every respect for many years. It has had an effective and stable board and management team over the past 30 to 40 years.

But when the CEO looked at the current situation—economic, social, financial, operational, clinical—he saw that everything has changed and he knew that his healthcare organization needed to change as well. The system would not be able to return to profitability just by doing the same things it would have done five years or 10 years ago. Instead of looking at a small number of factors and making incremental improvements, he wanted to look across the total enterprise all at once. And to look at all aspects of the enterprise with an eye toward organizational renovation.

I said, "So, you want a makeover."

The CEO is right. In an environment unlike anything any of us have experienced, and in an industry of complex interdependencies, the only way to get back to financial equilibrium is to take a comprehensive, holistic view of our organizations and environments, and to be open to an outcome in which we do things very differently.

In other words, a makeover.

Consider just a few areas that the hospital makeover could and should address:

There's the revenue side: Getting paid for what you are doing and the severity of the patient you are treating—which requires a focus on clinical documentation improvement and core revenue cycle delivery—and looking for any material revenue diversification opportunities.

There is the relationship with payers: Involving a mix of growth, disruption, and optimization strategies to increase payments, grow share of wallet, or develop new revenue streams.

There's the expense side: Optimizing workforce performance, focusing on care management and patient throughput, rethinking the shared services infrastructure, and realizing opportunities for savings in administrative services, purchased services, and the supply chain. While these have been historic areas of focus, organizations must move from an episodic to a constant, ongoing approach.

There's the balance sheet: Establishing a parallel balance sheet strategy that will create the bridge across the operational makeover by reconfiguring invested assets and capital structure, repositioning the real estate portfolio, and optimizing liquidity management and treasury operations.

There is network redesign: Ensuring that the services offered across the network are delivered efficiently and that each market and asset is optimized; reducing redundancy, increasing quality, and improving financial performance.

There is a whole concept around portfolio optimization: Developing a deep understanding of how the various components of your business perform, and how to optimize, scale back, or partner to drive further value and operational performance.

Incrementalism is a long-held business approach in healthcare, and for good reason. Any prominent change has the potential to affect the health of communities and those changes must be considered carefully to ensure that any outcome of those changes is a positive one. Any ill-considered action could have unintended consequences for any of a hospital's many constituencies.

But today, incrementalism is both unrealistic and insufficient. Just for starters, healthcare executive teams must recognize that back-office expenses are having a significant and negative impact on the ability of hospitals to make a sufficient operating margin. And also, healthcare executive teams must further realize that the old concept of "all things to all people" is literally bringing parts of the hospital industry toward bankruptcy.

As I described in a previous blog post, healthcare comprises some of the most wicked problems in our society—problems that are complex, that have no clear solution, and for which a solution intended to fix one aspect of a problem may well make other aspects worse.[1]

The very nature of wicked problems argues for the kind of comprehensive approach that the CEO of this organization is taking—not tackling one issue at a time in linear fashion but making a sophisticated assessment of multiple solutions and studying their potential interdependencies, interactions, and intertwined effects.

My colleague Eric Jordahl has noted that "reverting to a 2019 world is not going to happen, which means that restructuring is the only option.... Where we are is not sustainable and waiting for a reversion is a rapidly decaying option."[2]

The very nature of the socioeconomic environment makes doing nothing or taking an incremental approach untenable. It is clearly beyond time for the hospital industry makeover.

References

1 Kaufman, K.: "Healthcare's Wicked Problems." Kaufman Hall, Apr. 26, 2023.

2 Jordahl. E.: "The Balance Sheet Bridge." Kaufman Hall, May 13, 2023.

Re-setting the Healthcare Gyroscope

JULY 7, 2021

Every healthcare organization, large or small, depends on an internal gyroscope to assure its organizational stability and maintain its administrative and clinical navigation systems. That healthcare gyroscope is a delicate combination of management, governance, and medical attitudes and processes that keeps all complex healthcare organizations functioning in a way that serves the best interests of its patients and associated communities.

The COVID pandemic has impacted every aspect of our society in ways that we immediately understand and in other ways that it may take years and years to comprehend. In this regard, no institution may have been more emotionally and managerially impacted by the pandemic than the American hospital. That healthcare gyroscope in many healthcare providers has likely been knocked on its side and is now uselessly spinning sending the organization off in haphazard directions.

In the post-pandemic period healthcare leaders need to locate the most necessary set of strategic and operating plans which will most immediately re-establish that internal healthcare gyroscope. Here are a handful of suggested strategies that may prove most essential.

Consumer-centricity. Over the past 10 years, Big Tech moved the consumer to the very center of the economic competitive model. But the pandemic pushed that consumer-centric model to an even more prominent and unexpected level. Consumer centricity is now the essential basis for economic competition. Speed to market is clearly the critical component of corporate success. For healthcare organizations, customer-centricity will translate to a "simple" digital system of care that will allow patients to easily navigate their journey from diagnosis to treatment to recovery. Every American provider should assume that patients will aggressively migrate to the "easiest" healthcare solution available.

Operating efficiency. Continuous improvement in long-term cost structure and market share is necessary to generate sufficient margin and access to capital. Going forward, operating efficiency is likely to pivot around the following key objectives:

- Seek the lowest cost possible for all transactional functions
- Aggressively push toward paths for product and service improvement
- Maximize organic revenue growth
- Streamline the corporate structure by eliminating unnecessary entities, boards and committees
- Align capital allocation to high priority strategies and goals

Value-based care strategies. The pandemic highlighted the inexorable movement from fee-for-service to value-based payments. The rotation to value-based payments is moving at different speeds in different markets. Your payment product portfolio must not fall behind the pace of change in your particular market or markets. In this regard, double-down on the size and quality of your primary care network in order to support developing value based care options. And enter into the insurance marketplace in a way that is consistent with the size and financial capability of your organization.

Workforce development strategies. A combination of the pandemic and what is referred to as the 4th industrial revolution has turned workforce issues into perhaps management's most pressing long-term problem. Necessary clinical and administrative transformation will significantly change both traditional workforce roles and the attitudes and desires of the workforce itself. To properly prepare for the hard problems ahead, think of the following. First, identify areas of high workforce demand and make plans to meet that demand, and second, develop formal employee re-skilling programs offering career changes for impacted staff. Finally, give much thought to how the culture of your hospital matches up to the very difficult decisions around the developing hybrid office/remote work environment.

The healthcare environment has never been static. But change has been incremental and to a great extent predictable. The COVID pandemic has brought new, unpredictable external forces to healthcare that have already begun to affect the nature of healthcare's competitive dynamic and accelerate the pace of change. To weather this new environment, healthcare organizations need to achieve a new basis of stability. The above four strategies and their associated day-to-day tactics are just the beginning of the post-pandemic re-set for American healthcare providers. But together they can combine to set that organizational gyroscope spinning back toward governance, managerial, and clinical stability.

The Changing Business Principles in American Healthcare

APRIL 27, 2021

For a very long time, hospitals have been organized around three principles that inform the way they run their organizations, and how they conduct themselves in the management suite and the board room.

The first principle is the desire to **maintain organizational control**.

This principle has come about in large part because the clinical enterprise is inherently risky. Therefore, leaders do not want to be in a position where they don't have control of the clinical enterprise. That principle has extended beyond specifically clinical matters to all aspects of operation. Maintaining organizational control has come to mean minimizing organizational risk.

The second principle, which goes along with the first, is to **minimize enterprise risk**.

Hospitals have always been very risk-averse organizations. Over time, as different concepts have been introduced, organizations have had to be talked into doing things that allowed more risk, and that could result in better financial results from that risk or better strategic results from that risk.

The third principle is **maintaining operational flexibility**. Management teams and boards don't want to get caught in a box when difficult or bad things start to happen. This has to do with the public and reputational notion of running a hospital. Management and boards want to have the operational flexibility to take the actions necessary to resolve any situation that could harm the reputation of the organization.

These three principles are all well and good, but they have to be maintained and enforced. And it is expensive to maintain control, minimize risk, and maintain maximum operating flexibility. In general, leaders may believe that these very high levels of healthcare cost come from the way provider organizations are run. But that's not true. Leaders make decisions every day in which they actually pay to allow those three principles to be in full flight.

Let's look at a metaphor for this situation. If an organization is focused on maintaining control and eliminating to the greatest extent possible the externalities that limit control and increase risk, then when it comes time to finance, that organization will tend to look toward a 30-year fixed-rate transaction, because that transaction eliminates the risks of externalities.

However, if an organization wants to lower the costs of that transaction, the organization would do a variable-rate transaction or use certain hedging strategies. But getting those lower costs invites in the externalities of the world—the kind of externalities we saw in 2008 and 2009.

So management teams and boards that don't want to bring in those externalities look toward a 30-year fixed rate transaction at a higher cost.

This is a metaphor for all the other operating decisions that a hospital makes. If an organization's approach is to eliminate risk to the degree possible, and the leaders apply that approach to all their decisions, then the organization can purchase that increased control and minimized risk. But those decisions will result in higher costs.

We have recognized for many years that not-for-profit health-care is expensive. There is a fundamental philosophical reason for that situation. Organizations are trying to maximize the principles of maintaining control, minimizing risk, and maximizing flexibility, and they are paying up to do that.

There are hundreds of examples of situations in which organizations have to decide: Do we enforce these three principles? Or do we back off these three principles in order to reduce the overall costs of running the organization?

However, if we continue to proceed on this operating philosophy, we will continue to have the high operating costs that are directly correlated with that operating philosophy. If we want to get to a healthcare system that has a different operating cost point, then we have to rethink these operating principles.

Also, these operating principles create a perspective in which the needs of the organization are given a higher priority than the consumer's needs. That's the opposite of what a company like Amazon does. Amazon's mantra is, first figure out what the consumer needs, and then figure out what Amazon does.

When you insist on organizational control and low enterprise risk, the decisions that are being made in the board room are being made on behalf of the organization, and never really on behalf of the consumer. And that's a very unfortunate competitive place to be right now. This is just not the way the American economic model works anymore. The dominant model is the way that Apple, Microsoft, and Amazon behave every day. And in the past year, the dominance of that model has dramatically accelerated.

Now, in order for healthcare organizations to take advantage of certain critical opportunities, they are going to have to accept less control, to take more risk, and to reduce their operating flexibility.

In particular, that will be necessary in order to reduce cost materially. We've picked almost all the low-hanging fruit when it comes to costs, but costs are still too high. And that's because now we have to attack the operating principles in order to reduce costs more.

Next, hospitals will need to take a truly consumer-first attitude. Research shows that what consumers really care about is how they feel as they walk away from the interaction. Not how they felt when they first got there. Not how they felt while the transaction was happening. It's how they feel about the last mile. This has not been an area of focus for healthcare organizations. That last mile may be smooth from the hospital's perspective, but is the consumer truly happy when the encounter ends? For a company like Amazon, there is an extraordinary focus on making that last mile better and then better still.

The changing American economic model is incredibly fluid right now. It's highly dependent on technical competency and accumulated intellectual capital. Why has Amazon been so extraordinarily effective during the pandemic? Because they accumulated this extraordinary technical competency and this unbelievable intellectual capital, and then they were able to combine that competency and capital, and roll it out during the pandemic.

And that was what consumers wanted. Which is why Amazon's revenue was up 40% in the first quarter of the pandemic and while performance metrics fell through the floor for businesses using traditional business models, or businesses without the necessary technical competency and intellectual capital.

Hospitals don't have the technical competency and accumulated intellectual capital to be truly competitive in the dominant economic model. So hospitals will need to be open and experimental about possible partnerships and joint ventures to get that technical competency and intellectual capital.

There are so many strategic needs and opportunities in health-care now. The need to deliver a better experience to consumers. The need to reduce operating costs. The need to integrate digital health into the care process. It's naïve to expect that the average American hospital could do all these things themselves, which means that there are going to be many kinds of joint ventures and partnerships to accomplish these things. But in order to do those partnerships and joint ventures, it's inevitable that hospitals will have to accept less control and take much more risk, and accept reduced flexibility.

Observations on Management

DECEMBER 3, 2020

Those of you who regularly read this column know that earlier this year we discussed Jim Collins' four principles for managing during the COVID crisis. As a reminder, those principles were readiness, discipline, competitive separation, and lastly a transactional culture vs. a relationship culture. I am guessing that most readers found the first three principles fairly straightforward, but the concept of transactional vs. relationship cultures much more nuanced.

I think what Jim Collins was suggesting is that in recent decades, corporate and healthcare America have pivoted sharply toward a business culture that is transactional at its core and, at the same time, has de-valued a business culture based on traditional relationships. This observation is impossible to deny. In this economic era, America's most successful companies are built on a virtual, and by definition, transactional platform. And competitive pressures being what they are, this forces all companies toward that same transactional platform.

But what Collins is suggesting is that in a crisis, the most durable business culture, both internally and externally, is one built around relationships rather than transactions. Essentially, this concept suggests that, in a crisis, a transactional culture will fray while necessary strength will come from critical relationships among a healthcare organization's leadership team and board, and between the organization and its employees, caretakers, vendors, payers, regulators, governmental entities, and various communities.

Recently I was reviewing these Collins principles and concepts in some depth during a presentation, when a hospital CEO made an important clarifying point followed by a remarkably relevant question.

The observation was that healthcare organizations have rotated toward a transactional operating platform because that platform is highly correlated to efficient operations, consistent levels of clinical care, and excellent financial performance. The implication of the comment was that if an organization pivoted away from this transactional culture, then financial performance would accordingly suffer and suffer at a time when any healthcare organization could least afford such a downturn.

Over the years, Jim Collins has presented executives with so many essential and perplexing questions. And here is another. Is the transactional culture vs. the relationship culture an either/or proposition?

I will offer a commentary although I am sure that Mr. Collins will provide further insight in his writing still to come.

I would suggest that for strong, well-balanced, and high-performing healthcare organizations, these business cultures are not mutually exclusive. Rather, high-performing organizations recognize that in certain business environments a transactional culture will dominate, but in other environments, such as the COVID pandemic, that culture will be less effective. Faced with a black swan event (two in the last 10 years), a strong organization, with well-balanced leadership and governance, would be able to retain its transactional discipline, while at the same time activating critical relationships that are essential to first-class crisis management.

As I write this column, the pandemic has evolved to its absolute worst phase. More cases, more hospitalizations, and more deaths. Yet every day America's hospitals answer the call. Every day hospitals bring the necessary clinical, scientific, and intellectual resources to the fight to take the best possible care of our country in its time of greatest need. As described above, making the very best management and governing decisions is a pre-condition of that fight, and steering your organization's culture to exactly the right spot is a first principle to assuring your hospital's post-COVID success.

Financial Challenges for Healthcare Organizations

Revisiting the Importance of Financial Planning

MARCH 13, 2024

B etween 1987 and the early 1990s, Kaufman Hall created a formal corporate financial planning process designed specifically for not-for-profit hospitals. We recognized at the time that many not-for-profit hospitals were getting larger and more complex and that what passed for financial planning at the time was no more than reimbursement planning or budgeting—neither of which had the theoretical capability of solving complicated financial planning questions.

We didn't create this financial planning process out of thin air. Many of us at Kaufman Hall were graduates of the University of Chicago Graduate School of Business (GSB), now known as Booth. The essential principles of corporate finance had been developed and articulated at the GSB, most notably by James H. Lorie. Lorie, through corporate finance, had introduced a new series of methods of running large-scale corporations and organized that methodology around the investment principle, the financing principle, and the dividend principle. At Kaufman Hall, we took Lorie's theory and principles and adapted those principles to the unique planning needs of the not-for-profit hospital sector. In that regard, we started to prepare financial plans for clients in the late 1980s, and in 2024, we continue to build financial plans for the hospital industry and the methodology and theory behind our proprietary planning process has not changed in any consequential way.

I was reminded of all of this when I read that Richard Gonzalez was retiring from AbbVie as President and Chief Executive Officer. Gonzalez was the founding CEO of AbbVie and the company has been spectacularly successful under his leadership. But what was more interesting than Gonzalez's retirement was the appointment of his successor. The new CEO will be Robert Michael, who is currently the Chief Operating Officer at AbbVie. Notably, Michael began his career at AbbVie as Vice President of Financial Planning and Analysis. According to Crain's, he established and led AbbVie's first financial planning organization. It is significant that an executive who started out as a financial planner could eventually rise to become that organization's CEO. The fact that this is possible is an indication of how important the financial planning process is within the corporate for-profit business world. But it is also a powerful reminder that corporate financial planning should be given the same priority within the not-for-profit hospital universe.

All of this is to say that sophisticated financial planning remains the backbone for the management of complex organizations of any type or stripe. In the 1980s and 1990s, I wrote extensively about the theory and practice of corporate financial planning, but it is always a good time for an updated tutorial. To do that, I went back and read sections of a book written in 1994 by myself and Mark Hall. The book was entitled *The Financially Competitive Healthcare Organization*. It outlined a whole series of corporate finance skills and methods, but with special attention to financial planning best practices. Some key excerpts, still astonishingly relevant today, are as follows:

Management understands and applies principles of corporate finance. Consider again the difficulty of financial decision-making in healthcare today, and the high cost of mistakes in an environment of such complexity and uncertainty. How do financially capable organizations cope? They begin by building upon the strongest of foundations: the principles of corporate finance.

The capable organization seeks order. Order in this case can be defined as the use of consistent techniques to analyze and evaluate complex business problems. The principles of corporate finance impose mathematical order over essentially chaotic decision-making. A net present value analysis, for example, distills all of an investment's characteristics down to a simple dollar value, enabling the organization to evaluate the investment on its own merits or to properly compare it with other investment opportunities.

Remember: every decision an organization makes either adds to or reduces the value of the overall operation. The cumulative effect of these incremental decisions determines the organization's future financial success. Application of the principles of corporate finance enables the organization to measure the impact of each decision.

Given a technically capable finance department, senior management can aggressively incorporate analyses into the decision-making process and the board can depend on the numbers to validate the organization's key strategic moves.

Management has a sophisticated financial plan. The financial plan is the backbone of the financially capable healthcare organization. Not to be confused with the budget, which is the annual plan that allocates human and capital resources, the financial plan quantitatively evaluates the organization's financial risk given alternative scenarios. The sophisticated financial plan identifies corrective actions that the organization can make in response to certain expected or unexpected changes.

In business, as in sports, the team that best executes its plan is usually the winner. A sophisticated financial planning process enables the capable healthcare organization to execute. Logical and informed financial decisions give an organization the competitive edge in a marketplace whose changing needs demand quick response. Internally, a good financial plan lends the overall strategic plan a sharper focus and stronger momentum by bridging the gap between strategies and actions.

Management consistently applies quantitative decision-support tools. The financially capable organization distrusts intuitive solutions to complex business problems. This does not mean that the capable organization is afraid to make intuitive decisions but that it prefers to give its decision-making team a sound analytical footing on which to work. The executive team is comfortable with a wide variety of decision-support tools and is able to routinely prepare detailed financial projections for the organization as a whole and for the specific problem at hand.

The financially capable organization also employs a highly integrated planning process that instantly can show the financial impacts of changes to the strategic plan. This real-time decision-support structure allows for immediate analysis, consistent and reliable feedback, and improved communication, all prerequisites for first-class financial decision-making in our turbulent healthcare environment.

The above thoughts were written in 1994, and obviously times change and circumstances change. But the essential questions that underpin your analytic process do not change. Those questions are as follows:

1. What is the ambition of your organization as it relates to financial success, clinical growth, and improvement in reputation?
2. Based on the answer to question number 1, what would be the total required resources to achieve said financial success, clinical growth, and improvement in reputation?

3. Based on the five-year financial plan, is your organization on track to produce those resources as a combination of cash flow from operations, capital capacity, and possible philanthropy?

4. If not, what is the total shortfall in financial and capital capacity and are there operating and financial strategies available to close that shortfall?

The concluding observation from the 1994 financial planning chapter has not changed at all:

> The point is that the application of intuition plus experience without the benefit of analysis is just guessing, but the use of quantitative techniques without the buffer of experience and judgment is a meaningless mathematical exercise. Sophisticated financial planning creates a necessary and consistent context for able decision-making, despite uncertain and complex circumstances, and permits the informed application of executive judgment.

Corporate finance is a theory and methodology that has stood the test of time. It is perhaps the single most effective long-term technique to manage technically complex organizations. If all of this appears entirely obvious to Richard Gonzalez and Robert Michael at AbbVie, it should appear obvious to America's hospitals as well.

The Numbers Behind
the Numbers

FEBRUARY 21, 2024

With Erik Swanson, Senior Vice President, Kaufman Hall

We at Kaufman Hall do many interesting things. But among the most interesting is the publication of our monthly *National Hospital Flash Report*. We have the great fortune of receiving monthly financial information from hospitals throughout the country, which we translate into reports that summarize the financial status of the hospital industry on a monthly and an ongoing basis. The *Flash Report* has become the bible of macro hospital financial reporting and is relied on by hospitals, state hospital associations, and media outlets across the country.

While the *Flash Report* includes many charts and accompanying interpretive explanations, the chart that stands out over time is on page 90.

This chart demonstrates the roller coaster ride of hospital financial results between the end of calendar year 2021 and the end of calendar year 2023. The observations and questions from this chart are both interesting and required reading for hospital executives:

- Why were hospitals profitable at the 4% plus level through the worst of the 2021 COVID period?

- What exactly happened between December of 2021 and January of 2022 that resulted in a profitability decrease from a positive 4.2% to a negative 3.4%?

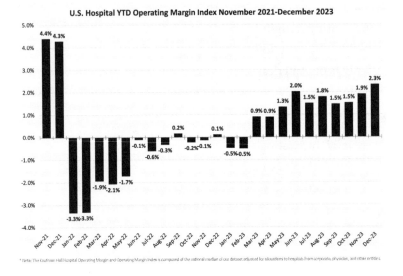

U.S. Hospital YTD Operating Margin Index November 2021-December 2023

* Note: The Kaufman Hall Hospital Operating Margin and Operating Margin Index is composed of the national median of our dataset adjusted for allocations to hospitals from corporate, physician, and other entities.

- Despite the best efforts of hospital executives, overall operating margins were negative throughout calendar year 2022 and did not return to positive territory until March of 2023.
- Hospital margins remained positive throughout 2023 and into 2024. However, overall margins have remained below those experienced in both 2021 and in the pre-COVID year of 2019.

The above questions and observations have proven interesting, and the ongoing numbers have proven quite useful in many quarters of healthcare. But recently I was talking with Erik Swanson, who is the leader of the Kaufman Hall *Flash Report* and our executive behind the data, numbers, and statistics. Erik and I were speculating about all of the above observations, but our key speculation was whether the 2023 operating margin results actually reflected a hospital financial turnaround or, in fact, were there "numbers behind the numbers" that told a different and much more nuanced story. So Erik and I asked different questions and took a much deeper dive into the *Flash Report* numbers. The results of that dive were quite telling:

Too many hospitals are still losing money. Despite the fact that the Operating Margin Index median for 2023 and into 2024 was over 2%, when you look harder at the *Flash Report* data, you find that 40% of American hospitals continue to lose money from operations into 2024.

There is a group of hospitals that have substantially recovered financially. Interestingly, the data shows over time that the high-performing hospitals in the country are doing better and better. They are effectively pulling away from the pack.

This leads to the key question: Why are high-performing hospitals doing better? It turns out that several key strategic and managerial moves are responsible for high-performing hospitals' better and growing operating profitability:

- *Outpatient revenue.* Hospitals with higher and accelerating outpatient revenue were, in general, more profitable.

- *Contract labor.* Hospitals that have lowered their percentage of contract labor most quickly are now showing better operating profitability.

- *An important managerial fact.* The *Flash Report* found that hospitals with aggressive reductions in contract labor were also correlated to rising wage rates for full-time employees. In other words, rising wage rates have appeared to attract and retain full-time staff which, in turn, has allowed those hospitals to reduce contract labor more quickly, all of which has led to higher profitability.

- *Average length of stay.* No surprise here. A lower average length of stay is correlated to improved profitability. Those hospitals that have hyper-focused on patient throughput, which has led to appropriate and prompt patient discharge, have also proven this to be a positive financial strategy.

Lower financial performers have financially stagnated throughout the pandemic. The data shows that throughout the pandemic, hospitals with good financial results improved those results, but of more consequence, hospitals with poor financial performance saw that performance worsen. The *Flash Report* documents that the poorest financially performing hospitals currently show negative operating margins ranging from negative 4% to negative 19%. Continuation of this level of financial performance is not only unsustainable but also makes crucial re-investment in community healthcare impossible.

The urban hospital/rural hospital myth. A popular and often quoted hospital comparison is that there is an observable financial divide between urban and rural hospitals. Erik Swanson and I found that recent data does not support this common perception. When you compare "all rurals" to "all urbans" on the basis of average operating margin, no statistically significant difference emerges. However, what does emerge—and is a very important statistical observation—is that the lowest performing 20% of rural hospitals are, in fact, generating much lower margins then their urban counterparts this year. It is at this lowest level of rural hospital performance where the real damage is being done.

Rural hospitals and obstetrics. The data does confirm one very important American healthcare issue: Obstetrics and delivery services are one of the leading money losers of all hospital service offerings. And the data further confirms that rural hospitals are closing obstetric departments with more frequency in order to protect the financial viability of the overall rural hospital enterprise. This is a health policy issue of major and growing consequence.

The point here is that data, numbers, and statistics matter both to setting long-term social health policy agendas and to the strategic management of complex provider organizations. But the other point is that the quality and depth of the analysis is an equally important part of the process. A first glance at the numbers may suggest one set of outcomes. However, a deeper, more careful and penetrating analysis may reveal critical quantitative conclusions that are much more telling and sophisticated and can accurately guide first-class organizational decision-making. Hopefully the analytics here are a good example of this very point.

Comments on Current Management Issues in the Healthcare C-Suite: Hospital Strategy and Planning in Times of Financial Challenge

AUGUST 7, 2023

think it is the general rule of thumb that during times of financial downturns hospitals tend to aggressively cut back on both planning and the execution of overall strategy. This approach seems to make governance and management sense: why would your organization spend future dollars when present dollars and current profitability are dramatically challenged?

Circumstances in the post-COVID era appear to be no different. How do we know? In the first half of calendar year 2019 total hospital debt issuance was $12 billion. In the first half of calendar year 2022 total hospital debt issued was $19.3 billion. Financial performance across the hospital board in 2022 was "awful" and by the second half of calendar 2022, total hospital debt issued was only $9.6 billion and the amount of debt issued in the first half of calendar 2023 fell further to $8.7 billion.

If you believe, as I do, that the absolute amount of hospital planning and strategy execution is highly correlated to total hospital debt issued, then we can conclude that hospitals post-COVID have significantly de-emphasized planning and strategy. As noted, this approach would certainly be expected based upon previous historical experience but is it the right road for hospitals to take at this time?

In fact, I do want to suggest in this blog post that the relationship between the COVID-induced financial downturn and the total attention to current hospital planning and strategy is different in substance now and should be approached differently by both the C-suite and by Boards. A few observations follow to encourage the discussion:

The COVID destruction of strategic relevance. One prominent CEO in the Southeast told me that post-COVID there was nothing relevant left from his 2019 strategic plan. This is an important point. In past financial turndowns hospitals could afford to ride out the immediate future with a "less than adequate" strategic plan. But my guess is that, like my friend in the Southeast, many hospitals now find their strategic plans are no longer "very strategic" and hardly "plans" at all.

The vision question. I would maintain that successfully navigating out from under the COVID downturn will require individual organizations to make a long series of financial, strategic, and clinical decisions. Another of my CEO friends suggests that managing through such financially distressed complexity first requires a corporate vision and, in fact, currently calls into question how many hospital organizations have emerged from COVID with an intact vision that is still understood by employees, managers, clinicians, and Board members alike?

Strategic investment. Many hospital organizations lost significant competitive ground during the pandemic. Failure to invest right now, failure to plan right now, all accompanied by a reluctance to issue additional debt poses the imminent risk of losing further ground in a healthcare marketplace that seems more random and disorganized every day.

Counterintuitive strategic aggressiveness. Is it possible that maintaining usual levels of investment during this post-COVID period in both planning and strategic execution is the best way forward? Can aggressiveness lead to competitive advantage and set the stage for a future increase in market share? Maybe those questions don't have actionable answers in the immediate moment, but it is, I think, important not to take such strategic aggressiveness off the management agenda prematurely.

Making hard decisions under uncertainty is the management dynamic of the moment in American healthcare. Unexpectedly, I found this very point illuminated by the poet James McMichael by way of the poet Robert Hass in his collection of essays, *Twentieth Century Pleasures: Prose on Poetry.*[1]

"Volition is, of course, what is wanted if one is going to combat uncertainties....And planning, McMichael reminds us, is the main human embodiment of will. Its purpose is to allay anxiety by showing us how we are going to get there. In fact...planning and anxiety are almost Siamese twins. It is when we are anxious that we start to plan."

There is little doubt that anxiety is the emotion of the moment in hospital conference rooms and Board rooms. And as McMichael and Hass sagely note, only ongoing and intelligent and determined planning can bring that anxiety under organizational control.

References

[1] Hass, R.: *Twentieth Century Pleasures: Prose on Poetry*. Ecco Press, 2023.

When Financial Performance Matters

NOVEMBER 21, 2022

n behavioral economics, the *sunk cost fallacy* describes the tendency to carry on with a project or investment past the point where cold logic would suggest it is not working out. Given human nature, the existence of the sunk cost fallacy is not surprising. The more resources—time, money, emotions—we devote to an effort, the more we want it succeed, especially when the cause is an important one.

Under normal circumstances, the sunk cost fallacy might qualify as an interesting but not especially important economic theory. But at the moment, given that 2022 will likely be the worst financial year for hospitals since 2008 and given that the hospital revenue/expense relationship seems to be entirely broken, there is little that is theoretical about the sunk cost fallacy. Instead, the sunk cost fallacy becomes one of the most important action ideas in the hospital industry's absolutely necessary financial recovery.

Historically, cases of the sunk cost fallacy can be relatively easy to spot. However, in real time, cases can be hard to identify and even harder to act on. For hospital organizations that are subsidizing underperforming assets, identifying and acting on these cases is now essential to the financial health of most hospital enterprises.

For example, perhaps the asset that is underperforming is a hospital acquired by a health system. (Although this same concept could apply to a service line or a related service such as a skilled nursing facility, ambulatory surgery center, or imaging center.) The costs associated with integrating an acquired hospital into a health system are typically significant. And chances are, if the hospital was struggling prior to the acquisition, the purchaser made substantial capital investments to improve the performance.

As time goes on, if the financial performance of the entity in question continues to fall short, hospital executives may be reluctant to divest the asset because of their heavy investment in it. This understandable tendency can lead the acquiring organization to throw good money after bad. After all, even when an asset is underperforming, it can't be allowed to deteriorate. In the case of hospitals, that's not just a matter of keeping weeds from sprouting in the parking lot. The health system often winds up supporting an underperforming hospital with both working capital and physical capital, which compounds the losses.

And the costs don't stop there, because other assets in the system are supporting the underperforming asset. This de facto cross-subsidy has been commonplace in hospital organizations for decades. Such a cross subsidy was probably never sustainable, but it is even less so in the current challenging financial environment.

This is a transformative period in American healthcare, when hospital organizations are faced with the need to fundamentally reinvent themselves both financially and clinically. The opportunity costs of supporting assets that don't have an appropriate return are uniquely high in such an environment. This is true whether the underperforming asset is a hospital in a smaller system, multiple hospitals in a larger system, or a service line within a hospital. The money that is being funneled off to support underperforming assets may be better directed, for example, toward realigning the organization's portfolio away from inpatient care and toward growth strategies. In some cases, the resources may be needed for more immediate purposes, such as improving cash flow to support mission priorities and avoiding downgrades of the organization's credit rating.

The underlying principle is straightforward: When a hospital supports too many low-performing assets, the capital allocation process becomes inefficient. Directing working capital and capital capacity toward assets that are dilutive to long-term financial success means that assets that are historically or potentially accretive don't receive the resources they need to grow and thrive. The underlying principle is a clear lose-lose.

In the highly challenging current environment, it is especially important for boards and management to recognize the sunk cost fallacy and determine the right size of their hospital organizations—both clinically and financially. Some leadership teams may determine that their organizations are too big, or too big in the wrong places, and need to be smaller in order to maximize clinical and balance-sheet strength. Other leadership teams may determine that their organizations are not large enough to compete effectively in their fast-changing markets or in a fast-changing economy.

Organizational scale is a strategy that must be carefully managed. A properly sized organization maximizes its chances of financial success in this very difficult inflationary period. Such an organization invests consistently in its best performing assets and reduces cross-subsidies to services and products that have outlived their opportunity for clinical or financial success.

Executives may see academic economic theory as arcane and not especially relevant. However, we have clearly entered a financial moment when paying attention to the sunk cost fallacy will be central to maintaining, or recovering, the financial, clinical, and mission strength of America's hospitals.

The Sobering State of Hospital Finances

DECEMBER 2, 2022

The American Hospital Association has released a report that we prepared for them on the state of hospital finances—and the results are sobering.[1] We are projecting 2022 to be the worst financial year for U.S. hospitals since the start of the COVID-19 pandemic. Our *optimistic* projections are for a 37% drop in operating margins, relative to pre-pandemic levels. Brace yourselves—our *pessimistic* projections show margins falling off a cliff with a possible 133% decline. And a growing number of hospitals are feeling the pain: More than half of all hospitals are projected to experience negative margins this year, up from 36% in 2021.

At this stage of the pandemic—late-stage, post, endemic, however you want to characterize it—battle-weary hospital executives would love to see macro-level financial projections heading in the right direction, if not returning to pre-pandemic baselines. But hospital costs have been rising as inflationary pressures, workforce shortages, supply chain disruptions, and drug expenses combine to drive up both labor and nonlabor expenses. Even in the few categories where expense growth is slowing, such as contract labor, costs remain far above pre-pandemic levels. To make matters worse, there is no additional federal financial support for hospitals in the foreseeable future.

So, how can healthcare leaders put these financial projections in perspective? Comparing current performance with the last pre-pandemic year provides essential information, but little reason for optimism. Unfortunately, reaching back to another time when hospitals experienced shared financial pain (albeit in very different circumstances) doesn't inspire hope either. The Great Recession of 2008, considered the longest period of economic decline since the 1930s, resulted in widespread investment losses, liquidity constraints, and technical defaults on debt covenants for hospitals. Hospitals had to restructure and resolve these problems, which by and large they did. But healthcare employment and national healthcare expenditures rose consistently during the Great Recession, despite substantial cuts in other sectors of the economy.[2] Profitability problems were not part of the recession picture for hospitals.

The reality is that the current financial condition of the hospital industry is worse than it was in 2008 at the peak of the Great Recession. The simple truth is that the pandemic and accompanying inflation have upended the longstanding relationships between hospital revenues and expenses. As a result, the pandemic cost structure of the hospital industry is operationally unsustainable. So, for better or worse, and like it or not, the strategic imperative right now is cost reduction.

As I said last year, the low-hanging fruit is gone.[3] Traditional approaches to cost reduction won't cut it. It's imperative to apply new and smarter approaches to this endeavor. Going forward, *every fiscal year* will likely require a measure of cost reduction. This macro strategy is especially difficult for not-for-profit hospitals because innovative, assertive, and necessary cost reduction pushes against longstanding cultural characteristics and risk tolerance for most such organizations.

Nevertheless, executives of leading healthcare systems realize that large-scale cost structure changes must be made. In recent conversations, several executives told me that they don't expect to be in a pre-pandemic revenue position anytime soon. As a result, they are grappling with major cost structure issues. And they are gearing up to make some tough decisions.

I'm often asked how permanent the current state of hospital finances will be. At this point, I think we can say that we are not going back to where we were in 2019. Our industry faces challenges that are structural in nature, not just cyclical (as with the economy) or situational (as with the pandemic). Are healthcare organizations that don't change their cost structure foreclosing on their own futures? We don't know the answer to that question. But the question must be raised and that, in itself, speaks volumes.

References

1 *The Current State of Hospital Finances: Fall 2022 Update*. Kaufman Hall & Associates, 2022.

2 Teasdale, B., Schulman, K.A.: "Are U.S. Hospitals Still 'Recession-proof'?" *New England Journal of Medicine*, Jul. 1, 2020.

3 Kaufman, K.: "Healthcare Costs Post-Pandemic: A Different Perspective." Kaufman Hall, Apr. 7, 2021.

Healthcare Costs Post-Pandemic: A Different Perspective

APRIL 7, 2021

With Lance Robinson, Managing Director, Kaufman Hall

For many hospitals and health systems around the country, COVID-19 threatens to create long-term negative changes to volumes, revenues, and margins on top of the pressures that weighed on hospitals even before the pandemic.

In January and February of 2021, adjusted discharges were down 17% and ED visits were down 28% compared with the same period in 2020, according to the latest Kaufman Hall Hospital Flash Report.[1] In addition, Kaufman Hall forecasts that hospital revenue could be down between $53 billion and $122 billion in 2021 compared with pre-pandemic levels.[2] We also forecast that median operating margins in 2021 could decline by 10% or greater from pre-pandemic levels, depending on the path of the virus and the ultimate effectiveness of the vaccine rollout.[3] By the end of 2021, we expect from one-third to one-half of U.S. hospitals to have negative operating margins. In addition, we are seeing significant changes in payer mix for some organizations, with greater percentages of government payers—another potential disruptor for margins.

Despite the volume and revenue blows that hospitals have felt, many have been reluctant to start aggressive cost control. In some cases, hospitals have expected—or at least hoped—that volumes and revenues would return to pre-pandemic levels, and in the meantime have leaned on their balance sheets and temporary government funding. Other hospitals are concerned about the possible ramifications of cost reduction at a time when COVID has already caused economic upheaval in their communities.

Given the nature of the problem, hospitals cannot wait much longer to recalibrate revenue and costs. At some point in the very near future, organizations need to come to a reckoning about the current state. What are current inpatient (medical and surgical), outpatient, and ED volumes; how do they compare with pre-pandemic levels; what are possible scenarios for the future? What has been the financial damage, with and without CARES Act funding? And is there a level of financial damage to the organization that appears to be permanent?

Any financial damage will have to be addressed: operating results will need to get back, if not to pre-COVID levels, to levels that are acceptable going forward.

As we have talked with hospital and health system executives around the country about this situation, a number of best practices for smart, assertive cost reduction have emerged that warrant serious leadership attention.

Update the financial plan. A foundational step is to update the organization's financial plan in order to determine cost goals over time. With the latest information on volumes, revenues, and expenses, along with scenarios about the path of COVID and possible changes in consumer behavior, executives need to extend the revenue line and the expense line over a period of years, absent any management action. What is the resulting gap between the organization's necessary financial state and what the plan shows?

Recognize that much of the low-hanging fruit has been picked. Hospitals have been toiling for years to reduce supply, labor, and overhead costs. In some cases, those costs have crept back in, and in some cases those opportunities have been achieved to a degree that is reasonable using traditional methods. On top of that, the new environment caused by COVID is changing the degree of cost reductions necessary. All these factors mean that new and smarter approaches to cost reduction are imperative.

Think of cost reduction as continuous. As executives look back at their organizations' financial histories and look forward at their financial plans, it will be apparent that one-time cost actions cannot do the job. *Every year* will likely require a measure of cost reduction. Therefore, plans should be designed from the start with the idea of being scalable for future requirements.

Focus on corporate overhead and shared services. During COVID, hospital front-line staff have carried an enormous burden of crushing hours, intense clinical uncertainty, personal sacrifices, and in many cases personal loss. As front-line staff continue to face the effects and unpredictability of COVID, and organizations look ahead to the workforce effects of burnout and the clinical needs for the next clinical crisis, executives are justifiably reluctant to reduce costs in a way that affects patient-facing staff. For that reason, in the face of continuing annual gaps in financial performance, executives should push as hard as possible on corporate overhead and—for systems—shared services.

Consider automation, outsourcing, and offshoring. As with other areas of cost reduction, traditional approaches to attacking overhead costs have yielded mixed results. Given the accelerating nature of the cost problem, organizations need to think more broadly about cost-reduction tactics. Among those that American corporations have used successfully for years are automation, outsourcing, and offshoring, specifically of *transactional* activities and functions—those that are rules based and repetitive. Examples include financial reporting, payroll, accounts payable, billing, insurance verification, and clinical documentation. Although not transactional, certain IT functions such as including desktop services, applications support, and coding work have a successful history of outsourcing in corporate environments.

Calculate and present the *full* opportunity. Organizations should start by calculating the full cost opportunity from a proposal that includes all strategies to their maximum effect. Then, without any alteration, this proposal should be presented to management. In effect, this approach says, "This is what we *could* do. Now tell us why we can't." Function leaders can review each area's cost-reduction strategies and, where necessary, the executive team may decide to postpone or phase in a particular strategy for a particular part of the organization. However, starting with the full opportunity helps manage the degree of change that will be necessary for these actions to be successful.

When outsourcing, consider the question of control. When outsourcing, two basic options exist regarding control. In one, the organization outsources a total function to a vendor, including leadership, design, and execution. In another option, the organization retains leadership and design, and outsources execution to a vendor. Neither approach is inherently right or wrong; both deserve serious management analysis and consideration.

Cost-reduction suggestions such as these push up against long-standing cultural characteristics of most not-for-profit healthcare organizations. For one, hospitals and health systems tend toward a desire to be all things to all people. These cost-savings approaches propose that certain functions can be done more effectively and efficiently by others.

An even more challenging cultural characteristic is not-for-profit healthcare's notorious aversion to risk. However, as one executive said to us, "In not-for-profit healthcare, risk-free cost-reduction plans don't exist anymore."

Innovative, assertive, and necessary cost reduction involves risk. Organizations need to ensure they have the right risk-mitigation strategies in place: for example, providing a safety net and retraining programs for displaced employees, or having an onshore backup for offshored functions.

With appropriate risk management in place, management and boards need to accept that a certain amount of risk is inevitable. There will be pitfalls along the way. However, if an organization is going to make the necessary adjustments to its cost structure on a recurring basis, bold moves are needed. Those moves are reasonable, given the opportunity. And they are necessary, given the alternative.

Traditional cost reduction strategies work on the premise that hospitals and health systems can lower their costs while maintaining full control of all aspects of operations, and that having full control lowers perceived risk. For the low-hanging fruit of cost reduction, that was largely true. At this point, however, maintaining that same level of control increasingly will mean that costs will be higher. For the next generation of cost reduction, most hospitals and health systems will have to accept something less than total control, and something greater than no perceived risk, in order to achieve their critical organizational goals over time.

References

1   *National Hospital Flash Report Summary: March 2021*. Kaufman Hall & Associates, 2021.
2   *COVID-19 in 2021: The Potential Effect on Hospital Revenues*. Kaufman Hall & Associates, 2021.
3   *COVID-19 in 2021: The Potential Effect on Hospital Revenues*. Kaufman Hall & Associates, 2021.

Getting Hospitals Back to their Fighting Weight

JUNE 2, 2020

The more we learn about the revenue shock that hospitals are experiencing from COVID-19, the clearer it becomes that recovering from that shock will require a rethinking of hospital operations.

The numbers are not pretty. In April, with a full month of COVID patients and shutdown of non-urgent services, hospitals' outpatient revenue fell 49%, inpatient revenue dropped 25%, and operating EBITDA margins fell 174%.

How quickly revenue will come back is anyone's guess. Anecdotally, we have seen surgical cases coming back quickly in some facilities, but continued major gaps in ED visits and in-person clinic visits. And COVID cases continue to increase in some markets, including spikes where stay-at-home orders are being lifted.

This is not the kind of shock that organizations can solve by staying the course. Even under the best scenarios, hospitals are facing unprecedented losses, with just guesses that business will return to pre-COVID levels within the next 12 months.

As we look out at the available information, it seems that over next 90 days or so hospitals will likely need to make major changes to operations in order to adjust to a loss of revenue whose exact level remains unknown.

To meet these fast-arriving cost and revenue challenges, hospitals will need to start with informed answers to fundamental questions.

First, we all need to be very clear about what high performance looks like. What are the core functions that must remain? What are the desired outcomes of those functions? What are the most effective structures within which to achieve those outcomes? What are the most efficient processes to carry out the functions? What is the optimal workforce for a new level of work? What technology support is needed? What facility arrangement is ideal?

Next, hospitals will need to honestly identify performance challenges. Where does the current structure create bottlenecks? Where are efforts duplicated? Where does communication break down? Which processes are problem-prone or poorly understood? Where are desired outcomes routinely not achieved? Which processes do not add value? Which functions are performed in multiple sites with varying levels of quality? Would these functions ideally be consolidated?

In addition, hospitals need to identify the lessons they have learned from COVID about operations. What changes did the organization make that brought positive results? Were certain functions paused that turned out not to add value? Did having staff work remotely reveal potential efficiencies? Could the organization reconfigure facilities for greater safety, better patient experience, and lower capital and operating costs? Will a shift in consumer demand require a realignment of administrative and clinical services?

Even tougher than answering these questions will be taking action based on the answers. However, basic math provides the impetus.

Executives I have spoken to, even at organizations expecting a strong return of patients, anticipate a long-term reduction in revenue. Assuming that revenues return to 95% of what they were previously, costs would need to be reduced by far more and far more quickly than traditional targets. And if revenues return to only 90% of previous levels, then the cost challenges escalate dramatically.

None of this is going to be fun. But we all just discovered how important our hospitals are to America's public health in the worst of circumstances. The COVID future remains uncertain. And importantly, many non-COVID patients need care as soon as possible. It is therefore critical that America's hospitals return to their fighting weight as immediately as can be managed.

The Economy of Disruption

The "Productization" of Healthcare Is Not Kind to Hospitals

FEBRUARY 1, 2023

For hospital providers across the country, the year 2022 was a big mess. A Kaufman Hall report prepared for the American Hospital Association predicts that 55% of hospitals will lose money from operations in 2022. And hospital margins have fallen by 31% from 2019 pre-pandemic levels. A very common question from hospital executives and board members alike is, "What happened? How and why did we fall from financial grace?"

The most obvious answer is that the critical relationship between revenue and expenses is unexpectedly broken. Inpatient revenue is flat, leading to year-over-year increase of net operating revenue of only 3%. Expenses, on the other hand, have increased by 8% in the past year, with labor expenses up, since 2019, by a remarkable 23%.

As usual, statistics tell the story, but they don't tell the entire story. The hospital industry is, for sure, bedeviled by a revenue-statement problem, but the range of operating and strategic problems within hospitals is much more nuanced.

One particular problem worth focusing on is what I call the "productization" of healthcare.

Historically hospitals offered what was loosely referred to as "healthcare," which meant a series of diagnostic and treatment services for which there was sufficient patient demand from an associated market area. Those services could be occasionally connected into a "center" concept, with mammograms, breast surgery, and oncology being one example. In other situations, hospital services could be discrete and disconnected, and often developed from a particular physician's unique expertise. But in no case were these connected or disconnected services referred to as products or operated as products.

Fast forward to now, and pretty much everything in healthcare has been organized into what is commercially known as products. The healthcare product list is long and comprehensive. Some services that are now products include urgent care, mammography, dermatology, ambulatory surgery, imaging centers, Walmart primary care, Walgreens primary care, and CVS primary care. That list is off the top of my head, but I am sure my reading audience can add many others to the "product" list.

Given the unsettled hospital environment, both financially and clinically, it is abundantly clear that hospitals struggle in a "productized" marketplace. Products require careful construction, and they require sophisticated and very close management. Products tend to operate as their own brand or under the aegis of a larger brand. Products tend to have close and individual financial management, because they tend to financially succeed or fail on their own.

All of this is counter-intuitive to many hospitals. Hospitals lean toward managing a patient population, and then selected services are enlisted for the benefit of those patients. Hospitals have "brands," but their services generally don't. Management is very sophisticated within the hospital ecosystem, but that management approach is generally operated with the entire enterprise in mind.

And finally, while more and more hospitals have capable cost accounting systems in place, hospital financial management tends to operate as a complex web of cross-subsidies based on profitable and unprofitable services, all operating on top of an ever changing payer mix. Such a financial structure was never designed to compete within a corporate or entrepreneurial product-centered market.

Hospitals are suffering in a "productized" world. As more and more so-called services are segregated into discrete products by larger corporations, by start-ups, and by private equity and venture capital, it seems inevitable that hospitals are losing traditional utilization and the financial rewards of that utilization. The statistics are not yet available to definitively prove this point, but the financial chaos of 2022 certainly suggests that hospitals find themselves at a significant competitive disadvantage in our fast changing "productized" healthcare world.

The Funnel Business Model of the Internet

JUNE 20, 2019

As I speak with healthcare executives around the country, I get many questions about the CVS Health/Aetna and UnitedHealth/Optum business models.

The questions have intensified with two recent announcements. UnitedHealth Group CEO David Wichmann said that Optum plans to grow from $16 billion to $100 billion annual revenue by 2028, and will do that without building any hospitals.[1] A few days later, CVS announced that it would expand its three-store HealthHUB pilot into 1,500 locations by 2021. HealthHUB is CVS's in-store health and primary-care experience.[2]

The best way to explain the growth strategies of these two companies—and the implications for hospitals—is by examining that I call the "funnel business model" of the internet economy.

This business model asks four basic questions:

- How many people potentially could be in your company's funnel?
- How broad is the top of your funnel as an entry point for these people?
- How do you get people into the funnel?
- How do you create the greatest number of interactions and transactions for people once they are inside the funnel?

Steve Jobs was a pioneer of the funnel business model in the early days of the internet. His vision was that almost any person or company with an interest in information, interaction, or media was a potential participant in the Apple funnel. The top of the Apple funnel was very broad, with devices from desktop computers to iPods. Apple attracted people into the funnel with products that were so intuitive and elegant that they became status symbols. And inside the funnel, the compatible and interconnected nature of the devices, along with a sizable content library, created multiple opportunities for further transactions.

At Amazon, Jeff Bezos has taken the funnel business model to an entirely new place.

How many people could be inside the Amazon funnel? Basically anyone. Not only does Amazon offer a mind-boggling number of products, but it also offers a broad array of highly desirable personal and business services, including cloud hosting and fulfillment. In addition, Amazon's platform that is so technologically advanced that it allows almost an infinite number of people to be in the platform at any given time.

Amazon attracts people into the platform with unmatched first-mile and last-mile experiences—the ability to find and select products easily and to get them into the hands of consumers rapidly. Inside the funnel, Amazon's extraordinary algorithms, Prime subscription service, and cross-marketing offer limitless opportunities for complementary transactions. Almost any click generates additional revenue for Amazon.

In short, Bezos' genius has been to create an extremely broad top of the funnel, to make it extremely attractive to enter the funnel, and to offer seemingly infinite opportunities within the funnel

The funnel is the internet business model that both United/Optum and CVS/Aetna are using.

For United/Optum, the top of the funnel is very broad: it extends to consumers, employers, and providers throughout the country and overseas, with a focus on developing concentrated services in 75 markets.

People are drawn into the funnel via about 50 million UnitedHealth memberships;[3] about 45,000 employed physicians;[4] and Optum services provided to four out of five U.S. hospitals, more than 67,000 pharmacies, and more than 100,000 physicians, practices, and other health care facilities.[5]

Inside the funnel, United/Optum offers an incredibly broad collection of interrelated services for individuals, employers, and healthcare providers, including insurance, population health management, ambulatory surgery, primary care, occupational care, urgent care, pharmacy benefit services, and analytics.[6]

For United/Optum, hospital services are not seen as something that adds much breadth to the top of the funnel or that draws people into the funnel—certainly not enough to justify Optum taking on the high fixed costs and poor pricing of inpatient care. Rather, hospitals are an additional interaction within the funnel that can be accomplished through partnerships rather than ownership, according to Wichmann. Those partnerships, he says, "will occur in markets where there is maybe less assets for us to accumulate and build from."

United/Optum is largely focused on adapting the traditional healthcare delivery and insurance system to the funnel business model. CVS/Aetna, on the other hand, is taking a bolder approach.

CVS is creating an even broader top of the funnel. The CVS funnel targets practically any consumer—someone wanting to fill a prescription, take a yoga class, or buy a bag of potato chips.

The entrance to the CVS funnel combines a massive physical footprint with a growing digital presence. CVS has about 10,000 retail stores. Eighty percent of Americans live within 10 miles of a

CVS store. With the expansion of CVS's HealthHUBs to 1,500 locations, one analysis suggests that 75 percent of Americans would live within 10 miles of a HealthHUB.[7] In addition, CVS/Aetna has access to about 18 million Aetna medical insurance members in all 50 states.[8] On the digital front, CVS has 62 million loyalty program members whose purchasing patterns can be tracked and who can be the target of tailored promotions.[9]

Inside the funnel, CVS is aiming to create large collections of products and services pertaining to health and wellness that combine in-person and digital interactions. These include retail products organized around health themes (for example, pregnancy or healthy diets); in-person experiences such as yoga and exercise; digital engagement through education and wellness apps; assistance with insurance navigation; wellness services such as nutrition counseling and sleep assessments; and low-intensity healthcare services including immunizations, physicals, routine primary care, and chronic care. CVS plans to expand its digital care services, particularly through in-home monitoring.

United/Optum appears well on the way to making its version of the funnel business model a success. For CVS/Aetna, the jury is still out, but the company's strategy has been very carefully created and aligns with other successful business models of the internet economy.

The funnel business model is a reality for healthcare. For hospitals, the question is not if but how to participate. For some, participation will include building or rethinking their own funnel. For others, participation will mean partnering with other companies.

Capital, scale, and technological capabilities clearly will be requirements for hospitals to succeed. More important, however, will be a new way of thinking about several foundational issues.

One is **intellectual capital**. Hospitals will need people who speak the language of the total market served, who are steeped in contemporary means of personal and commercial interaction, and who have a demonstrated ability to draw traffic and create a first-class consumer experience. These individuals need to be given sufficient position and authority to truly influence how a hospital interacts with all the people it touches.

Another is a **new approach to interaction**. Organizations will need to look beyond traditional inpatient and outpatient care when they think about interaction with consumers. They will need to look at all the personal and commercial activities of their consumers, to find ways to become part of those activities, and to ensure that health-related interaction is continuous, not episodic.

Finally, hospitals will need to think about their **relationship with consumers** in a new way. In the internet economy, the traditional paternalistic viewpoint of healthcare providers toward patients will only attract people in times of specific need. To make an organization the destination of choice requires a relationship of mutual respect. It requires a deep understanding of consumers' experiences within and beyond healthcare. It requires a fierce dedication to the highest level of service. And it requires creativity to design the kind of interactions that will delight and even surprise consumers.

Traditionally, hospitals do have a funnel. They touch many people in a community and offer many interrelated services. However, speed and scale are coin of the realm in the internet economy. So it's no surprise that new entrants in healthcare are aiming to take the healthcare funnel to a new level—to create a funnel that is exponentially broader, more attractive, and more engaging. For these new entrants, the funnel business model is deeply embedded in organizational culture, capabilities, and strategies. Virtually every major business decision these companies make has the goal of achieving a more active funnel. For hospitals to be a competitive force at the top of the funnel, they will need to have this same strategic orientation and discipline.

References

1   Pflanzer, L.R.: "UnitedHealth is Already the Biggest US Health Insurer. Now It Wants to Make Going to the Doctor Its Next $100 Billion Business." *Business Insider*, May 31, 2019.

2   "CVS Health Announces Significant Expansion of HealthHUB to Deliver a Differentiated, Consumer Health Experience." CVS Health press release, Jun. 4, 2019.

3   Masterson, L.: "UnitedHealth Sees Membership, Revenue Up in Q1." *Healthcare Dive*, Apr. 17, 2018.

4   Stone, J.: "UnitedHealth Group Soon to Be Largest Employer of Doctors in the US; Clinical Laboratory Outreach More Critical than Ever Before." *Dark Daily*, Jun. 29, 2018.

5   Optum: Overview." UnitedHealth Group

6   Byers, J.: "Optum a Step Ahead in Vertical Integration Frenzy," *Healthcare Dive*, Apr. 12, 2018.

7   Tully, S.: "CVS Wants to Make Your Drugstore Your Doctor." *Forbes*, May 17, 2019.

8   Norris, L.: "How to Choose the Best Health Insurance Plan." *Very Well Health*, Mar. 6, 2024.

9   "About CVS Health." CVS Health.

Metallic Blue Cars

MAY 1, 2019

Since the mid-1960s, Cosmopolitan magazine has been well known for its iconic covers: stunning models or celebrities in front of solid-colored backgrounds surrounded by provocative cover lines. Prior to that time, Cosmo was a staid, moderately successful literary magazine. In 1965, Helen Gurley Brown took over the magazine, identifying a new kind of modern reader and discovering "there were millions of her."[1] The most visible manifestation of this new approach was the bold covers.

Today, Cosmopolitan has a new Editor-in-Chief—32-year-old Jessica Pels, who was the subject of a recent *New York Times* profile.[2] Pels has a degree in film and video production and was in charge of Cosmo's digital strategy for less than a year before becoming editor of the entire enterprise.

Pels doesn't observe the Cosmo reader; she *is* the Cosmo reader. She lives the life of her readers—at work, at home, in her social life, and perhaps most importantly, online. This complete identification with Cosmo's customers has led to Pels making a breakthrough observation about running a business today: *In order to understand consumers' commercial behavior, you must understand their personal behavior.*

In the past, the commercial fact base was the commercial behavior of the consumer population: Which products did consumers buy? How many products did they buy? Were consumers happy with the products? Would they recommend the products to others? Pels' realization is that now the fact base isn't the *commercial* behavior, it's the *totality* of consumers' behaviors.

Nowhere are those behaviors better demonstrated than on the platform where they play out: social media.

For Cosmo, Instagram is one of the best places to witness consumer behavior. Instagram has 1 billion active users[3] and a relatively affluent user base.[4] According to Pels, Cosmo's average reader opens Instagram 42 times per day.[5]

Instagram gives Cosmo an amazingly precise view of what is popular among its readers. Cosmo acts on that information directly and immediately. Vintage metallic blue cars began showing up everywhere on Instagram. The cover of Cosmo's April issue featured four actors in a vintage metallic blue car. Heart-shaped pizza was popular on Instagram. Heart-shaped pizza was featured in a March photo spread.

Having recognized the commercial importance of consumers' online personal lives, Cosmo has rapidly embraced the implications. A key implication is that Cosmo's magazine is no longer the core of its business. Cosmo's emphasis now is on new platforms and their revenue sources: Digital subscriptions have doubled in the past two years. Ecommerce revenue from affiliate vendors through the Cosmo site has doubled in the past year. Cosmo has 2.7 million followers and more than 7,000 posts on Instagram; it has 785,000 subscribers and more than 2,000 videos on its YouTube channel.

Cosmo's new point of view begs an important question for legacy healthcare organizations: What is the metallic blue car for healthcare?

What would happen if legacy healthcare providers were immersed in the totality of consumers' lives and used those insights to redefine the healthcare experience?

Now granted, many healthcare organizations are making moves in the direction of the metallic blue car. However, in Kaufman Hall's extensive consumer research, we continue to hear comments like these:

> *I have a health problem, but I don't know which kind of doctor to call.*

> *I know my provider has some sort of call-a-nurse service and some kind of online scheduling, but I don't know how to get to them.*

> *My provider's website is confusing.*

> *I hate making appointments over the phone.*

> *I wait a long time at the doctor's office, and it's the same experience I had 20 years ago, including the same magazines.*

> *I know I have a MyChart account, but I can't remember the web address or my password.*

> *I have to give the same long list of information to every doctor I see.*

> *My healthcare providers don't value my time.*

In a recent follow-up survey, we asked 2,000 consumers what type of company they would trust to develop the best online tool to help them find the right healthcare services. The top preference was a big tech company like Google, Amazon, and Apple. The second preference was an insurance company. The last preference was a hospital or health system.

Those responses should be both a warning and a rallying cry for all legacy healthcare organizations. No one knows what the metallic blue car is in healthcare. But it is up to America's hospitals and health systems to find it before consumers find it somewhere else.

References

1   Scutts, J.: "Helen Gurley Brown: Cosmo Editor's Quest for Glamour, Sex and Power." *The Guardian*, Jun. 8, 2016.

2   Rosman, K.: "At Cosmopolitan Magazine, Data Is the New Sex." *The New York Times*, Apr. 5, 2019.

3   "Most Popular Social Networks Worldwide as of April 2024, Ranked by Number of Monthly Active Users." Statista, 2024.

4   McLachlan, S. "35 Instagram Statistics That Matter to Marketers in 2024." HootSuite, Nov. 21, 2023.

5   Rosman, K.: "At Cosmopolitan Magazine, Data Is the New Sex." *The New York Times*, Apr. 5, 2019.

Now, Near, and Far: Planning Through Disruption in Healthcare

APRIL 17, 2019

To see the future of healthcare, look through the windshield of a Ford.

Within the past year, Ford Motor Company announced that it is terminating production on most lines of its passenger sedans to focus on higher-margin trucks and SUVs. In October, Ford announced that tariffs and trade tensions had cost it $1 billion in profit, and its stock price neared a nine-year low. It is in the midst of a $25.5 billion restructuring, and massive layoffs—up to an estimated 12 percent of its global workforce—are likely.[1] And it looks forward to a future where it sees demand for its current product much reduced.

Populations continue to migrate to congested urban centers. Ride-sharing services, motorized bikes, and electric scooters are challenging the traditional model of car ownership in these urban cores. Tech companies and Ford's auto industry competitors are racing to perfect the technology that could soon bring fleets of battery-powered, self-driving vehicles to the streets. Car making suddenly seems less relevant in a transportation future that will likely be defined by software and mobility service platforms.

Facing disruption of his company and industry, Ford Motors CEO Jim Hackett has turned to a framework he developed in his previous role as CEO of Steelcase. This framework challenges companies to work simultaneously in three time dimensions: the now, the near, and the far.

- **Now.** Be successful in the now and simultaneously make the critical pivot to the far. For Ford, this means ending sales of sedans in the U.S. to free up $8 billion to support investment in electric and autonomous vehicles.
- **Near.** Place bets on the future and pivot resources to support those bets. Ford will transform its remaining fleet of F-150s and SUVs into electric vehicles with autonomous features.
- **Far.** Envision a future state and future role, knowing that any prediction is uncertain and subject to change. Ford must develop the right portfolio to support multiple modes of transportation working together in connected, consumer-centric systems.

Even though Ford has developed a powerful intellectual and strategic framework to guide its transformation, it faces challenges of enormous complexity in making the pivot from now to far.

First, it must be able to look outside its current business and conceptualize a future that is radically different. The culture and talent required to succeed in the far also may be completely different from what is required in the now. There are many bets being placed in transportation and mobility services, but no one has a clear vision of what comes next. And a culture 100 years in the making can be difficult to change.

Second, it must get the timing right. People are not going to suddenly stop buying cars in favor of scooters—timing of the transition to the far will be uncertain. Moving too soon means sacrificing the profits still to be made in the now, and limiting the resources needed to invest in the near and far. Moving too late risks giving competitors the upper hand.

Third, the scale of the pivot needed to transition from the now to the far might simply exceed the financial and intellectual capital that Ford is able to bring to bear to support a new business model or out-compete a better equipped competitor. Ford faces competition not only from other automakers, which are facing the same pressures as Ford, but also by well-funded and technologically savvy competitors, including Alphabet and Uber.

The fate of one-time industry leaders such as Blockbuster, Borders, and Kodak illustrates the huge challenge companies face in reinventing themselves for an unpredictable future. These companies were unable to successfully respond to disruption not because of ineptitude, but because it is so difficult to focus simultaneously and successfully on three timeframes with three different requirements: now, near, and far.

The Now, Near, and Far in Healthcare

Legacy health systems face their own existential threats. Their business model developed around hospital-based services, and the intense financial and human capital needs of hospitals gave them some protection from competition. Health systems built networks of primary care physicians to help ensure a referral stream of patients needing higher acuity, hospital-based care. Advances in medicine and technology started to move care outside of the hospital walls. Health systems responded by building outpatient services bolted onto their core inpatient business. This is healthcare's "now."

The more care that can be removed from the high-cost hospital setting, the more it becomes open to competitors whose interest lies in unbolting primary care and outpatient services from the health system and providing it in low-cost, high-convenience settings—both physical and digital—that emphasize consumer experience. Low cost, convenience, and consumer experience are real vulnerabilities for legacy health systems. And if new markets entrants are successful in unbolting primary care and outpatient services, they also will gain significant influence over where patients needing higher acuity inpatient services go for their care. This is what health systems face in healthcare's "near."

Competitors are moving in on a healthcare industry that remains largely local and small in scale. Even though there has been much hospital and health system consolidation activity in recent years, even the largest health systems are dwarfed by the scale of new competitors that bring a national presence and exceptionally deep pockets to the table. The recent merger of CVS Health and Aetna created a company with $240 billion in combined revenue and 10,000 retail locations, described by CVS Health CEO Larry Merlo as a "new front door to healthcare."[2] UnitedHealth Group, with more than $201 billion in annual revenue for 2017, has targeted 75 markets across the country for expansion of primary care services through its Optum unit, which is positioning its digital health platform, Rally, as "our digital front door for the consumer."[3] In comparison, the largest health system in the country, for-profit HCA, has approximately $43 billion in annual revenue. On the not-for-profit side, the largest system, when merged, will be Dignity Health/Catholic Health Initiatives, with combined annual revenue of around $28 billion—roughly one-tenth the annual revenue of CVS/Aetna.

Although their plans are less certain, tech giants with even deeper pockets have strongly signaled their interest in moving into healthcare. Amazon has partnered with JPMorgan Chase and Berkshire Hathaway to take "a fresh approach" to healthcare. JPMorgan Chase CEO Jamie Dimon said, "We don't expect progress in the immediate future—like a year or two—but if we come up with some great stuff, we're going to share it with everybody."[4] Alphabet recently hired David Feinberg, who was CEO of Geisinger, one of the nation's leading health systems, to lead the various health initiatives that are being developed within Alphabet's Google unit. Apple is developing "AC Wellness" clinics that will initially serve its employee population, and released an updated version of its Apple Watch with an FDA-approved electrocardiogram monitor app. These companies will certainly be involved in shaping healthcare's "far."

Although the far is uncertain, legacy health systems have the advantage of hindsight in understanding what disruption might look like. When companies such as Optum and CVS talk about a "digital" or "new" front door to healthcare, they describe a fundamental part of the internet economy: the movement of services from an old platform (the retail store, the physician office) to a new platform. Amazon started by removing the sale of books from the physical platform of the bookstore to Amazon's website, which has since expanded exponentially to connect buyers and sellers across a vast array of products. Other companies have disrupted industries with digital platforms that connect consumers with service providers: Uber for ride-sharing, Airbnb for lodging, GrubHub for restaurant meals.

Once a digital platform has been built, it can be scaled up at little cost and expanded into other services. Uber, for example, wants to become "the Amazon of transportation"[5] by developing a multi-modal transportation platform to compete in the same area of mobility services that legacy auto makers envision as their "far." It has already added electric-assisted bikes and scooters to the transportation options that can be accessed through the Uber app.

An emphasis on convenience, access, and experience is shared across the platforms of digital disruptors. Very few of them produce the "content" (the products or services) that is offered on their platforms, at least initially. Instead, they focus on making the connection between consumer and content as seamless as possible. In doing so, they generate intense customer loyalty, which drives more and more transaction volume on their platforms. Increasingly, web- or app-based platforms are becoming the basis of a broader ecosystem as voice recognition technology and digital assistants proliferate in consumers' homes, automobiles, and devices. Platform owners also are expanding their ecosystems back into physical locations reimagined to seamlessly connect with their digital services (for example, Amazon's acquisition of Whole Foods, which now offers in-store deals to Amazon Prime members).

Legacy companies within the disrupted industry see the strength of the old platform—the stores where products were sold, the city streets where cab rides were hailed—weaken as more transactions move to the disruptor's new platform. They must compete by supplying content on the disruptor's platform, creating or collaborating with an alternative platform that competes with the disruptor, or some combination of these options.

Competition among content providers on a disruptor's platform also commoditizes the product or service that the content providers offer. A content provider thus must compete on the price of the commoditized content or demonstrate some other value that appeals to consumers.

While not all healthcare services will move to a digital platform, disruptive innovators will be testing the limits of which services can be delivered digitally. Digital platforms will also be introduced to disrupt the means by which consumers connect with providers of healthcare services. Platforms will feature round-the-clock access and capacity that is scalable to meet demand. To the extent the digital platform becomes a "front door" to the healthcare system, the platform owner gains influence over the consumer's subsequent healthcare choices. These choices might include retail locations, ambulatory surgery centers, or other sites of care also controlled by the platform owner or a partner organization within a broader ecosystem accessed through the platform.

Platforms might be owned and operated by health systems, health plans, or new market entrants. They might seek to disrupt legacy organizations' existing business models, seek to collaborate with legacy organizations, or both. They might focus on niche services or connect consumers with a full range of healthcare providers and services. These are among the uncertainties of how healthcare's "far" will unfold. But the "far" requires health systems' attention now.

Figure 1: Now, Near, and Far for American Healthcare

Now	Near	Far
Complete ownership of inpatient care	Continued consolidation, with average transaction size growing	Division between platform owners and content providers
Robust and profitable outpatient segment bolted on to inpatient model	Division of industry into more distinct groups of inpatient or outpatient providers	Movement of outpatient services to digital platforms
Geographic and face-to-face orientation	New entrants (e.g., Optum, CVS, Amazon) focused exclusively on outpatient services	Build-out of broader ecosystem that enable multiple points of access to care, controlled by the platform owner or partner organization
Revenue pressure from payers	Legacy health systems forced to defend profitable outpatient flank while continuing to support inpatient flank	Platform owner influences consumers' content choices
Struggle to manage costs	Diminishing inpatient volumes	Hospitals are cost centers
Largest systems at $10-$20B in revenue	National health systems form to compete with new entrants	A few platform owners compete on a regional or national basis

Finding a Role in the Far

Health systems already face the now and the near outlined in Figure One: they must simultaneously prepare for the far. Their first step is to define the organization's desired role in the far, which may include being a content provider, owning a platform, or some combination of the two. If they choose to be a content provider, they must also decide what will make them an *indispensable* content provider. If they choose to be a platform owner, they must decide whether they will go it alone or collaborate with other companies.

An organization's decision on its desired role will be driven by multiple factors (see Figure 2). Will it focus on a local market or operate on a larger regional or national stage? Will it offer broad-based or more specialized services? What are its points of differentiation from a consumer perspective? To what extent has it already experimented with value-based payment and care delivery models? What relationship would it want in a new, platform-based healthcare economy? Answers to these questions will differ widely among different organizations. But all must place bets on the future and their desired role in it.

Becoming an indispensable content provider.

Content providers in a platform-based vision of healthcare's far will be in a position similar to a vendor on Amazon's retail platform. And like these vendors, the greatest risk healthcare organizations will face as content providers on a platform is the risk of commoditization. They must consider how they will differentiate themselves from other content providers, and how these points of differentiation will make them indispensable to both the platform owner and the consumers it serves.

Becoming indispensable depends on the organization's ability to differentiate itself from its competitors, and price, quality,

Figure 2: Factors Influencing the Desired Role of a Hospital or Health System

Market and Geography	Service Focus	Points of Differentiation	Value-Based Payment Position	Relationship with New Platforms
Local	Niche	Cost	Wait and see	Participant
Regional	Broad-based	Quality	Testing	Partner
Statewide	Tertiary/complex	Access	Catalyst	Developer
Multi-state	Outpatient-focused	Experience		
National				

convenience, and experience will all be points of differentiation. An organization's success as content provider, however, will ultimately be defined by the consumer's preference for the content provided on one platform over another. Simply being a content provider on any platform will not be enough: Organizations must be sensitive to which platforms are preferred by consumers and work to differentiate themselves sufficiently both to secure a role as content provider on the consumer-preferred platform and to be a preferred content provider on that platform.

Becoming a Platform Owner

This is a significantly more resource-intensive role, which will require both a large financial investment to develop the platform and sophisticated in-house technical and digital capabilities. Given the resources required to build a platform capable of competing with other platform companies, which will likely operate on a regional or national scale, this option will be difficult to achieve, even for large health systems that have a strong regional or national presence.

Organizations that pursue a platform ownership strategy may decide they can develop sufficient resources to go it alone, or they may seek to collaborate or partner with another organization. For example, a health system could partner with larger platforms to augment the services it is able to provide in its market. Already, some health systems have partnered with national telehealth providers, such as MDLIVE and American Well, to offer white-labeled telemedicine platforms that provide after-hour services or can reach more remote patient populations.

The decision to become a content provider or platform is not necessarily an either/or choice. Organizations may decide that the best strategy is a combination of approaches. In retail, some companies have built their own platform that features the full range of their services, and have offered a more limited inventory as a content provider on another platform. Tiffany's sells the full range of its products on the company's own platform, but offers a more limited selection on the luxury fashion platform, Net-a-Porter. Similarly, a health system may develop a platform that provides access to a full range of services for consumers in its primary service area, but feature specific, highly-rated specialties on a third-party platform that operates on a wider regional or national basis.

Addressing the Capabilities Gap

Once a health system has defined its desired role for the far, it will likely run up against a hard reality: few health systems today have anything near the capabilities they will need to succeed in the far, regardless of their desired role. In a recent survey of the state of consumerism in healthcare, only 23 percent of respondents said they were using digital tools to engage consumers, and an even lower number—17 percent—reported that e-visits were widely available for consumers. In the words of one survey respondent:

"The traditional healthcare industry is so far behind in terms of meeting, much less anticipating, consumers' expectations, that I fear for our ability to adapt quickly enough to remain relevant."[6]

Adapting quickly to build the capabilities needed to succeed in the far is one of the most difficult challenges health systems face. Many capabilities will be required. Those that will present the greatest challenges include:

- **Digital capabilities:** The availability of features such as online scheduling services, telemedicine and other virtual care options, and patient access to their medical records and test results will be table stakes for all health systems. Those that pursue a role as platform owner will need highly sophisticated capabilities to design, build, and maintain a digital platform, and will have to compete with others to secure this talent.

- **Access.** Consumers will expect access to facilities across the geography of a market, as well as access to virtual care or extended hour services at facilities. Both convenience and immediacy of access will be priorities. This will require staffing models and expectations for clinicians—including physicians—that are very different from today.

- **Consumer experience**. Long wait times, confusing billing statements, and a lack of transparency are all part of the consumer experience in healthcare's now. Health systems must learn to gather and act upon in-depth information about consumer preferences and expectations for when, where, and how they want they want to experience and engage with services and providers.

- **Cost performance.** Nearly one in three health system executives in a recent survey said there organization has established no cost-improvement goals for the next five years.[7] This is a recipe for disaster. Price will be a key differentiator, and those health systems that have not gotten serious about tackling their costs will be among the most vulnerable.

- **Financial position.** Health systems face competitors with massive financial resources at their disposal. One of the most compelling reasons to go after costs now is to build the balance sheet strength and access to capital needed to invest in the talent, digital technologies, and innovation that competition in the far will require.

- **Culture.** Risk aversion and incremental change will not take a health system where it needs to go. Leadership must build a culture that takes risks, fails fast, learns from its mistakes, and moves forward.

Health systems that make a frank assessment of where these capabilities currently stand will find significant gaps between the current state and future needs. If the gap between future need and current state is too great, or the health system believes that the time it will need to close the gap is too long, it may need to reexamine its desired role. More importantly, it needs to define its strategic priorities, identify the resources it needs to pursue them, and get started closing the capabilities gap now.

Mapping the Pivot from Now to Far

This is the biggest challenge health system leaders face: They must train their organization to look across the three time dimensions of now, near, and far simultaneously to stage its strategies, ensure its initiatives are driving toward a clear goal, and time its pivot from now to far.

Figure 3 shows how a health system that has placed its bets on the far might map its strategic priorities across the now and the near. There are no set time periods that define now, near, and

Figure 3: Mapping Progress Across the Now, Near, and Far

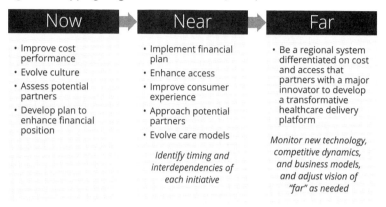

far. Different markets will likely vary in speed, and an unforeseen catalyst could easily accelerate the pace in a market that is currently moving slowly toward the far.

Organizations should nonetheless define at the outset what they believe are appropriate timeframes for the three dimensions, based on their assessment of the pace of disruption within their market and the time needed to close the gap between the current state of their capabilities and future needs. They should also recognize that the pace of change will require them to implement multiple strategic priorities simultaneously.

Each strategic priority must also be backed by specific initiatives to drive success and metrics to measure progress toward realizing the priority. Defining initiatives and metrics is, however, just a start. Health systems must be sensitive to several factors that might impede their progress or require them to change course.

Interdependencies of Initiatives

As a health system puts its initiatives into place, it also must step back and take a comprehensive view of initiatives across the organization. Where do lines of dependency between or across initiatives exist? To what extent is the completion of one initiative a precondition for the success of another? If one initiative fails, what will the impact be across other initiatives?

It is highly unlikely that any organization will be successful across all the initiatives in puts into place. Instead, success will depend on another interdependency: whether the organization has built a culture that can fail fast, learn from its mistakes, and move forward on a corrected course.

The Pull of the Now

One of the hardest forces for any company to escape is the pull of the now. There will always be a temptation to set aside work on a future that seems both distant and uncertain in favor of work that sustains a current business model. But doing so risks leaving an organization unprepared and overwhelmed when the gap between the now and the far closes.

Health systems can use several tactics to counter the pull of the now. They should define separate metrics that track progress toward near and far goals in the now. They should regularly monitor progress toward goals across all three dimensions. They should consider establishing separate teams dedicated to work on the near and the far who are kept free from the distractions of the now. And they should reward individuals accountable for achieving near and far goals in the same way that the reward individuals who achieve goals in the now.

A Changing Vision of the Far

As a health system becomes more invested in its commitment to pivot from the now to the far, its work will be complicated by the simple fact that the far will always be uncertain. Organizations must get comfortable with the idea that they cannot seek what does not exist.

Instead of seeking certainty, health systems must place bets on the uncertain, building both diligence and flexibility into their processes. They must regularly revisit their vision of the far and their desired role in it, and quickly make any needed adjustments to their desired role, strategic priorities, and initiatives if their vision of the far changes significantly.

Management guru Peter Drucker said, "The greatest danger in turbulent times is not the turbulence, but to act with yesterday's logic." The new logic for health systems is to look forward from the now to the far, charting a course that will meet the turbulence of disruption head on.

References

[1] Kelleher, K.: "Ford Prepares for Mass Layoffs After Losing $1 Billion to Trump's Trade Tariffs, Report Says." *Fortune*, Oct. 10, 2018.

[2] De la Merced, M., Abelson, R.: "CVS to Buy Aetna for $69 Billion in a Deal that May Reshape the Health Industry." *The New York Times*, Dec. 3, 2017.

[3] "United Health Group Inc. (UNH) CEO David Wichmann on Q2 2018 Results – Earnings Call Transcript." *Seeking Alpha*, July 17, 2018.

[4] Franck, T.: "Jamie Dimon Says Health Care Initiative with Buffett and Bezos May Start Small Like Amazon Did with Books before Expanding." CNBC, July 30, 2018.

[5] Kerr, D.: "Uber Wants to Be 'the Amazon of Transportation,'" *CNET*, Sept. 6, 2018.

[6] Crnkovich, P., Clarin, D., O'Riordan, J.: *2018 State of Consumerism in Healthcare: Activity in Search of Strategy*. Kaufman, Hall & Associates, 2018.

[7] Robinson, L., Fitz, T., Goetz, K., Seargeant, D.: *2018 State of Cost Transformation in U.S. Hospitals and Health Systems: Time for Big Steps*. Kaufman, Hall & Associates, 2018.

The Amazon Pinball Machine

DECEMBER 14, 2018

Your microwave may soon be letting you know when you need to order more popcorn. With the introduction this fall of a $60 microwave with an embedded connection to Echo and its Alexa voice recognition technology,[1] Amazon took another step toward immersing Echo users in an ecosystem in which their every request is monitored, responded to, and if possible, converted to a sale.

In the internet economy, an ecosystem is a contained system of consumers, products, and suppliers, with embedded triggers for interaction among them. It works like a pinball machine. Within the closed system of the machine, the pinball, once launched, darts from bumper to bumper, rolls down chutes, falls into holes and pops out, rewarding the player with blinking lights, bright sounds, and points. Some of the movement is created by the user's skill with flippers, but much of it is created by the internal workings of the game.

The most desirable pinball machines, the ones that draw the most people to launch that pinball, are the ones with the most immersive experience and the best rewards: the brightest lights, the most exciting movements, the most invigorating sounds, the longest play time, and the most points. The goal of the machine is not to facilitate any one instance of a ball setting off a light or sound, but to use many of these instances to draw more players to the machine.

Similarly, the goal of a business ecosystem is not any individual sale, but to create traffic. More traffic translates into more interactions, more information, more loyalty, more sales, and more opportunities for creative integration into people's lives.

Amazon is not interested in making money on microwaves. The company will gladly take a loss by selling a $60 microwave if that will bring more people into its ecosystem. Neither is Amazon interested in selling popcorn. That is just one more bright light to make the ecosystem appealing. The key is to establish a solid framework for the ecosystem; with that, it can be added to at will.

Ecosystems and the Internet Economy

The ability to create and grow ecosystems is a fundamental principle for success in the internet economy. The imperative to create an immersive ecosystem, where the consumer can interact independent of location or a particular device, has led to the tech giants' expansion into retail stores, automobiles, and the consumer's home, making the line between digital and physical environments increasingly irrelevant.

The Amazon ecosystem has become almost unimaginably pervasive. The broadest framework of the Amazon ecosystem is Prime. As of June 2018, Amazon had 95 million Prime members nationwide.[2] The company has raised the Prime membership price in the U.S. only twice since the program began in 2005,[3] but has worked overtime to enrich benefits, from free streaming video to two-hour grocery delivery from Whole Foods Markets.

Amazon also has developed highly innovative ways to enter and engage with its ecosystem. Amazon Echo can now connect with more than 20,000 smart home devices from 3,500 different brands.[4] Echo also is being built into center console displays of new Toyotas, BMWs, and Audis, or you can buy Alexa Auto for $50 to bring Alexa into your vehicle.[5]

Amazon is not the only game in the arcade. Its main rivals, Apple and Alphabet, also have developed ecosystems anchored by operating systems that bring seemingly limitless applications to their smartphones. Their initial strategy was to build an ecosystem around the device that travels with you throughout the day. They also have developed voice recognition technology (Siri and the Google Assistant) and are expanding the hardware options through which consumers can access their ecosystems. Google, in particular, has made significant inroads with its Google Home device. [6]

All three companies have managed to expand their ecosystems far beyond what any of them could do alone by making participation by third-party vendors inexpensive and easy. For a few dollars, Amazon offers manufacturers of electronics and home appliances a small chip that they can build into their products to connect with Alexa.[7] Apple and Alphabet have long provided open access to their operating systems to developers that want to develop apps for download or sale in the Apple or Android app stores. These same operating systems are now providing options for third parties to link with devices that are moving the companies' ecosystems into consumers' homes.[8]

All of this means that consumers are growing accustomed to finding more and more of what they want within their chosen ecosystem, and more and more ways to access what they want immediately, wherever they are.

Healthcare on the Table

In The Who's "Pinball Wizard," Tommy can "beat my best." As the tech giants eye healthcare, their skill in growing ecosystems that attract and retain consumers with seamless access to an increasingly vast range of services should give healthcare leaders pause.

It is no secret that the tech giants are very interested in healthcare. Both Apple[9] and Amazon[10] are reportedly developing new models for healthcare clinics, starting with their employee populations. Amazon has acquired online pharmacy PillPack,[11] and its joint venture with Berkshire Hathaway and JPMorgan Chase to reduce healthcare costs for the three companies' 1.2 million combined employees has drawn constant coverage since it was announced.[12]

Apple introduced significant upgrades to its Apple Watch in September that turn the watch into a health monitoring device, complete with an electrocardiogram monitor app that has received FDA approval.[13] And Alphabet recently convened its first healthcare conference for the various units across the company working on healthcare solutions in artificial intelligence, in-home monitoring, wearable devices, and anti-aging research—evidence of its intent to take a more focused approach to the healthcare space.[14]

David Feinberg recently announced that he is leaving his position as CEO of Geisinger Health System to lead Google's healthcare initiatives. A few weeks before the announcement, responding to the question of what kept him up at night as a health system CEO, he said: the fear that Google and Apple would "eat our lunch" at serving patients and being responsive to their needs.[15]

As consumers grow more familiar with and more immersed in the tech giants' ecosystems, finding healthcare as another service available to them within the ecosystem would feel completely natural. And if the tech companies offer healthcare with the same engaging experience that they offer for other services, accessing healthcare services within the consumer's chosen ecosystem could be as seamless as streaming a video or ordering more popcorn for the microwave are today.

Healthcare organizations have never faced competitors quite like Amazon, Alphabet, and Apple. One thing is certain: They play a mean pinball.

References

1 Haselton, T.: "I Tested Amazon's Super-Cheap Microwave That You Can Talk to, and It's Pretty Darn Good." CNBC, Nov. 14, 2019.

2 Coppola, D.: "Number of Amazon Prime Members in the United States as of December 2019." Statista, Jul. 14, 2023.

3 DePillis, L., Sherman, I.: "Amazon's Extraordinary Evolution." CNN, Oct. 4, 2018.

4 Green, D.: "Amazon's Latest Investment Hints at the Future of Alexa." *Business Insider*, Sept. 25, 2018.

5 Levy, N.: "Amazon Reveals Flurry of New Devices as Tech Giant Aims to get Alexa Inside Homes and Cars." GeekWire, Sept. 20, 2018.

6 Oremus, W.: "Alexa Is Losing Her Edge." *Slate*, Aug. 23, 2018.

7 Stevens, L.: "Amazon's New Microwave: 'Alexa, Please Defrost My Chicken.'" *The Wall Street Journal*, Sept. 20, 2018.

8 Jhonsa, E.: "Amazon Is Pulling Out All the Stops Against Apple and Google in the Voice Assistant Wars." *The Street*, Mar. 25, 2017.

9 Farr, C.: "Apple's First Hires For Its Health Clinics Show How It's Thinking Differently About Health Care." CNBC, Aug. 2, 2018.

10 Farr, C.: "Amazon Has Plans to Open Its Own Health Clinics for Seattle Employees." CNBC, Aug. 9, 2018.

11 Peebles, A., Hirsch, L.: "Amazon Shakes up Drugstore Business with Deal to Buy Online Pharmacy PillPack." CNBC, Jun. 28, 2018.

12 Abelson, R., Hsu, T.: "Amazon, Berkshire Hathaway and JPMorgan Name C.E.O. for Health Initiative." *The New York Times*, Jun. 20, 2018.

13 Gurman, M.: "Apple Gets FDA Approval for New Watch, Touts Health Gains." *Bloomberg*, Sept. 12, 2018.

14 Farr, C.: "Alphabet Kicks Off a Private Two-Day Conference Dedicated to Health, Featuring AI Chief Jeff Dean and Other Leaders from All Over the Company." CNBC, Nov. 6, 2018.

15 Diamond, D., via Twitter. Nov. 8, 2018.

Now, Near, and Far: A Lens for the Internet Economy

DECEMBER 7, 2018

t is tempting to disparage Blockbuster, Borders, and other companies that have suffered highly public business disruption at the hands of the internet economy. From the comfortable position of hindsight, it is hard to conceive that Blockbuster would not have understood that consumers would prefer streaming video to crowded parking lots and late fees, or that Borders would not have foreseen that Amazon's easy online ordering and near-infinite selection would decimate Borders' stores. Even more perplexing in hindsight is that, once the threat was obvious, Blockbuster and Borders did not act more decisively to stay relevant.

Yet, the fact that these companies were unable to successfully respond to disruption is not an indication of their ineptitude, but of the enormous complexity involved in reinventing their companies for an unpredictable future.

First, they needed to recognize a rapidly emerging and entirely new delivery and business model. It is hard to recall how novel e-commerce seemed in 1997, when Amazon was still just a book-seller,[1] or how novel streaming video seemed in 2007, when first launched by Netflix.[2] These were groundbreaking concepts whose business and social implications were hard to grasp and whose unprecedented rise was nearly impossible to predict.

Second, had they recognized the scope of the threat, leaders at Blockbuster and Borders would have needed to envision an entirely new role for their companies within a new business model. That role would have required entirely new capabilities, while many of the companies' existing characteristics—for example, a heavy real estate portfolio—would have been major impediments.

Third, Blockbuster and Borders would have needed to make a difficult pivot to this new, unknown role, redirecting significant portions of capital, rapidly acquiring new intellectual and technological capabilities, and transforming the companies' cultures.

Fourth, while this massive and rapid transformation was taking place, Blockbuster and Borders would have needed to maintain their high performance in the existing business model to have the financial strength to make the necessary transition.

In short, Blockbuster and Borders would have needed to focus simultaneously and successfully on three timeframes with three different requirements: *now, near,* and *far*.

Now, Near, and Far Defined

Jim Hackett, CEO of Ford Motor Company, developed the concept of "now, near, and far" while he was CEO of Steelcase. He insisted that now, near, and far were not a continuum, but three dimensions that required simultaneous and equal attention. As we gain more experience with disruption arising from the internet economy, we gain a more nuanced understanding of the interdependent and sometimes conflicting demands of these dimensions:

- **Now:** Be successful in the "now" while also making the critical pivot to the "far"
- **Near:** Place bets on the future and pivot resources to support those bets
- **Far:** Envision a future state and future role, knowing that any prediction is uncertain and subject to change

The now, near, and far framework is getting a major test as Ford confronts a new world of mobility, from self-driving cars to scooter sharing. Against a backdrop of weak sales and stock price, Ford finds itself needing to devote significant attention, resources, and creativity to now, near, and far simultaneously. For example:

- **Now:** Ending sales of sedans in the U.S.—frees up $7 billion to support electric and autonomous vehicles[3]
- **Near:** Transforming F-150s and SUVs into electric vehicles with autonomous features
- **Far:** Develop the right portfolio to support multiple modes of transportation working together in connected, consumer-centric systems

The Power of Now, Near, and Far

Blockbuster and Borders were understandably overwhelmed by the complexity of balancing now, near, and far. Those companies existed in a time when the five-year strategic plan of a successful company rarely called for its complete reinvention. The internet economy has changed all that. High-tech companies now compete for revolutionary ideas that will fuel rapid growth. This sets a pace that legacy companies struggle to match without major pivots in cultures, capabilities, and roles.

"Now, near, and far" is a powerful framework for organizing the complex options facing legacy companies in the internet economy. The framework allows executives and boards to isolate the specific strategies needed to succeed in the current business model, and to transition to a new business model. It allows executives to prioritize the strategies with the most direct impact on success in a new business model. It allows executives to manage the timing of those strategies as the organization pivots from the current business model to a new one. And it gives executives a simultaneous view of performance critical for success in all three dimensions.

In a recent issue of *The Wall Street Journal*, Ford took out a full-page advertisement with stark blue type on a white background. As these excerpts show, the ad expresses the critical balance of now, near, and far that could apply to legacy companies in any industry:

Now: "We are proud to be an automotive company." Near: "We have been thoughtfully and methodically making our way into the future for over a century." And far: "We believe in having the longest view in the room."

Ford's success in pivoting from "now" to "far" is by no means certain. The company is facing powerful headwinds of technological and socioeconomic change. In Ford's favor, however, is something that Blockbuster and Borders lacked: a powerful intellectual and strategic framework to guide its transformation.

References

1 DePillis, L., Sherman, I.: "Amazon's Extraordinary Evolution." CNN, Oct. 4, 2018.
2 "The Story of Netflix," Netflix.com.
3 "CEO Strategic Update," Ford Motor Company, Oct. 3, 2017.

Lower Forever

FEBRUARY 8, 2018

"Lower forever" is a term used inside oil giant Shell to describe future oil prices. Not "temporary downturn" or "entering a new cycle," but "lower forever."

The demand for fossil fuel is expected to peak as soon as 10 years from now. At that time, oil prices—and the industry they support—will begin to change forever, as described in an excellent Jan. 24, 2018, *Fortune* article by Jeffrey Ball titled "Inside Oil Giant Shell's Race to Remake Itself for a Low-Price World."[1]

The phrase "lower forever" has the virtue of brutal honesty. It shows that Shell accepts the existential threat that comes with a permanent reduction in demand for a company's core products. And it focuses the company on making foundational changes, rather than protecting the status quo or nibbling around the edges of change.

In another piece of brutal honesty, Shell's CEO admits, "We don't know anymore where the future will go." However, even lacking a specific destination, the company is aggressively taking steps that will reduce its risk, prepare for a new revenue model, and discover a new role. Those steps constitute a playbook for any organization facing permanent decline in its core business.

Avoid stranded assets. Shell is concerned that when oil prices decline, the company could be left with expensive assets that will not be sufficiently profitable and that no one will want to buy. The company is aggressively reviewing its portfolio and divesting these lower performing assets. For example, Shell recently sold most of its stake in a Canadian oil sands project for $7.25 billion.

Make major cuts in operating costs. No matter what role Shell plays in the future, it must ensure that it can maintain a sufficient margin as oil prices fall. Despite its current profitability, Shell has laid off 12 percent of its workforce, with more cuts to come.

Rethink current operations and products. Shell also is working to reduce its own carbon footprint (which currently is nearly as large as that of Germany) and to decrease the carbon content of its products, aiming for a 20 percent reduction by 2035.

Develop future scenarios. Shell has been hard at work analyzing potential changes in demand for various forms of energy and penetration of new technologies such as electric vehicles. High energy demand and low new-technology penetration would be the closest to the status quo. Low energy demand and high technology penetration would mean massive disruption for Shell.

Pick a path, make investments, and hedge your bets. Shell is placing bets on multiple approaches to clean energy, investing in wind and solar power, acquiring an electric-car-charging company and a British electricity company, and developing plants that can tap multiple energy sources. Shell is also making an investment in hydrogen as a future carrier for multiple forms of energy. As Shell's ultimate strategic path becomes clearer, it plans to significantly increase the related investments.

Legacy health systems find themselves in a position remarkably similar to that of Shell. Multiple forces are causing a decline in demand for core inpatient services and revenue for these services. We don't know exactly how quickly that decline will take place.

New approaches to care delivery—such as retail models and virtual care—and new players—such as UnitedHealthcare/Optum and CVS/Aetna—are emerging, but we do not know exactly what models and companies will predominate.

Occupying a position similar to that of Shell, hospitals and health systems can take away two major lessons from Shell's approach to "lower forever."

First, accept the inevitability of permanent change. Socioeconomic forces make major changes to our healthcare system inevitable. An acceptance of that inevitability has significant implications for organizational planning and strategy. Planning becomes less about modifying existing strategies and operations, and more about designing entirely new roles, revenue models, structures, and operations for a new environment.

Second, the specific future may be hazy, but actions can and must be taken immediately. We may not know the future specifically, but we know it directionally, and that direction is a decline in profitability for core services. The Shell example shows that meaningful actions can be taken even in absence of a certain future. Cost reduction is imperative for the inevitably downward direction of core revenue. Scenario development is imperative to shape strategic decisions. Coordinated and significant investments and participation in new care models provide important experience, as well as positioning organizations to take advantage of multiple opportunities.

Oil is a big, complex, capital-laden legacy business. Planning cycles for new initiatives can cover a decade or more. In an industry like that, a change coming as soon as 10 years from now requires immediate action. Shell has recognized that fact and is moving accordingly.

"Big, complex, and capital-laden" is an equally apt description of American healthcare. Like Shell, America's hospitals need to adopt a brutally honest view of the future and take the necessary actions to translate an acceptance of "lower forever" into a new business model that can handle a very uncertain future.

References

[1] Ball, J.: "Inside Oil Giant Shell's Race to Remake Itself for a Low-Price World." *Fortune*, Jan. 24, 2018.

Healthcare's Last Mile

DECEMBER 14, 2017

Amazon is experimenting with same-day delivery by drones, delivering packages inside your home even when you are away, and eliminating traditional check-out from retail stores. These are just the latest examples of how companies like Amazon, Google, and Uber continue to build their successes in an unending effort to make the "last mile" shorter and then shorter still.

The "last mile" refers to the final step by which consumers receive goods or services. Today, companies are focused on tackling the last mile in ways and with levels of convenience that were previously unimagined. Successful Internet-era companies are never satisfied with the level of convenience in the last mile: Five clicks could be three clicks; two-day delivery could be 30-minute delivery; opening an app could be a voice command; a product search could be anticipated by artificial intelligence. The race to find the most innovative ways to shorten the last mile is the race for dominance in the Internet economy. The same race will play a large role in the healthcare winners of the future.

Until recently, traversing the last mile has been largely the responsibility of the consumer: driving through traffic, finding parking, hailing taxis, waiting in lines, picking up packages at a post office, or hoping packages don't get stolen from the front porch. Consumers accepted this situation because few better options were available. Companies accepted this situation because changing it would be difficult and expensive, and change seemed unnecessary as long as consumers continued to tolerate their role.

In the Internet economy, however, consumers are learning that virtually any service can be accessed from your couch via smartphone or other voice-activated device. The result is intense competition among creative, aggressive, well-capitalized companies to develop the best platform to remove friction from the last mile for consumers. At the same time, legacy providers of goods and services need to determine the business implications of competing to fulfill these new consumer expectations.

Ignore, Compete, or Participate?

Food delivery is a prime example of the dynamics of last-mile competition. GrubHub, DoorDash, UberEats, and Amazon Restaurants are just a few of the services launched within the past two years to offer online ordering and fast delivery from restaurants, from fast food to high-end cuisine. Investment firm Cowen forecasts 79 percent growth in the total U.S. food delivery market between 2017 and 2022.[1] Morgan Stanley finds online orders to be more than 50 percent of the food delivery market and growing.[2]

Competition is intense among these online delivery platforms, with GrubHub recently being eclipsed by UberEats, due to Uber's user base, brand recognition, and logistics expertise.[3] The ultimate showdown to be the platform of choice likely will be among titans: Uber, Google, and Amazon.

For legacy restaurants, the rise of these delivery platforms poses a fundamental business question that will resonate within any industry experiencing disruption, including healthcare: *ignore, compete, or participate?*

Ignore. Restaurants that ignore the rise of digital delivery put themselves at considerable risk of business erosion. In essence, they are self-selecting out of the contemporary digital environment.

Compete. Only the largest chains have the scale and capital to develop a competing digital delivery service with anything close to the reach and performance of giants like Uber. One example is Domino's Pizza, whose historic value proposition has been delivery speed. Domino's moved early and aggressively toward developing digital capabilities, and in recent years has been called a tech company that makes pizza.[4] Domino's is well known for its Domino's Tracker, which allows people to follow their pizza from preparation to delivery, even purportedly naming the people who cook and deliver the pizza.

Participate. Most restaurants have little choice but to participate with multiple existing platforms, accepting the terms that those platforms set. Although this participation is a hedge against loss of relevance, it comes with costs, risks, and operational challenges.

The most obvious cost is the cut of revenue taken by delivery services, which is in the neighborhood of 20 percent.[5] Restaurateurs might hope that additional volume will make up for this revenue loss, but that is by no means a sure bet. These apps typically feature a huge number of restaurants with comparative consumer ratings, introducing more intense, data-fueled competition among participants.

Restaurants also are finding that their traditional operations need to be changed for an environment in which a growing percentage of patrons never enter the restaurant.[6] Some are developing menus with an eye toward food that travels well. Some are redesigning the packaging used for food delivery. Some are setting up separate work spaces to manage delivery orders. As time goes on, restaurants may even find that they do not need the same physical footprint or workforce configuration.

Reinventing Healthcare's Last Mile

This massive shift in food delivery arises from the desire to remove the relatively modest amount of friction involved in visiting a restaurant.

It's safe to say that healthcare's last mile has a bit more friction: Calling to make an appointment. Waiting days or weeks for that appointment. Taking off work for the appointment. Driving to, parking at, and finding the provider's office. Filling out paperwork—often multiple times. Waiting to be seen by the provider. Going to separate locations for lab tests, scans, or X-rays. Waiting to hear from the provider about the results. Visiting a provider to have a prescription refilled. Dealing with insurance approvals. Dealing with communication among providers. Accessing medical records. Understanding statements. Paying invoices.

On the last mile, legacy healthcare organizations are playing catch-up. Health systems are working on online scheduling, virtual visits, rapid retail clinics, and consumer-provider messaging. Yet, while healthcare is pursuing these fledgling efforts to remove friction from the healthcare experience, Amazon is developing stores that have no cashiers and no checkout lines, Google is developing self-driving cars, and Spotify is populating customized music playlists. Catching up with that level of innovation is daunting to say the least.

As is the case with digital ordering and food delivery, state-of-the-art convenience in healthcare's last mile requires a level of intellectual and financial capital that few organizations can access. Even the largest healthcare organizations are partnering with tech leaders on these initiatives. Such partnerships are not panaceas, however. Organizations need to have a clear understanding of how collaborating with other organizations for services such as urgent care, virtual visits, and precision medicine will affect volume, revenue, and consumer loyalty. The last outcome legacy healthcare organizations want is to find themselves a commodity service within a larger and more popular healthcare platform.

And such a platform may be coming. Amazon is reported to have a "secret skunkworks lab" exploring "a platform for electronic medical record data, telemedicine, and health apps for existing devices like the Amazon Echo."[7] Google recently launched Project Baseline to collect comprehensive health data in order to map disease and prevention.[8] Perhaps most telling, Apple recently explored acquiring two medical clinic chains, which would open the door to a very different and very scalable healthcare experience.[9]

Maintaining Loyalty

Legacy healthcare organizations enjoy an extraordinarily close connection with their communities. People identify with their providers based on years-long or generations-long relationships.

A San Francisco restaurateur recently noticed that "the faces we used to see day in and day out, we started to see less and less."[10] When he would run across one of the formerly familiar faces, he would ask, "Did we do something wrong? Why don't we see you as much anymore?" They would reply, "Oh, we're just ordering delivery now. The restaurants are so busy, we don't want to wait in line."

This anecdote contains a profound truth for healthcare providers—a truth that emerging nontraditional competitors understand very well. Healthcare providers need to recognize that their consumers may be loyal to a point, but that they are coming to expect a new kind of experience. To maintain that loyalty, providers will have to learn the lessons of Amazon, Google, and others, and make the last mile far, far easier to traverse.

References

1 Franck, T.: "Home Food Delivery is Surging Thanks to Ease of Online Ordering, New Study Shows." CNBC, Jul. 12, 2017.

2 "Alexa, What's for Dinner Tonight?" Morgan Stanley, Jul. 21, 2017.

3 Dixon. V.: "UberEats Is Destroying Your Favorite Delivery Service," *Eater*, May 9, 2017.

4 Beer, J.: "How Domino's Became a Tech Company." *Fast Company*, May 22, 2014.

5 Levy, S.: "DoorDash Wants to Own the Last Mile." *Wired*, Nov. 9, 2015.

6 Filloon, W.: "How Restaurants Are Adapting to the Food Delivery Boom." *Eater*, Sept. 18, 2017.

7 Kim, E., Farr, C.: "Amazon Has a Secret Health Tech Team Called 1492 Working on Medical Records, Virtual Doc Visits." CNBC, Jul. 27, 2017.

8 Farr, C.: "Alphabet Will Track Health Data of 10,000 Volunteers to 'Create a Map of Human Health.'" CNBC, Apr. 19, 2017.

9 Farr, C.: "Apple Explored Buying a Medical-Clinic Start-Up as Part of a Bigger Push Into Health Care." CNBC, Oct. 21, 2017.

10 Filloon, W.: "How Restaurants Are Adapting to the Food Delivery Boom." *Eater*, Sept. 18, 2017.

The Fresh Eyes of Disruption

DECEMBER 30, 2017

When people didn't return video rentals on time, Blockbuster saw that behavior from the perspective of a movie-rental company—as a problem to be fixed with late fees and changes to the rental period.

Netflix looked at that behavior from the point of view of the consumer—as evidence that people wanted a different, more flexible approach to home entertainment. Netflix used new technology to create a whole new kind of home-entertainment company. Blockbuster remained a movie-rental company until it was too late to change.

Opportunities for disruption are easy to see in hindsight, but extremely hard to see in the moment. Few companies have the curiosity, receptivity, and fearlessness to translate an observation about consumer behavior into a conclusion that a well-established company should change its core business. Yet those are the core capabilities required of companies seeking to stay ahead of disruption in the Internet economy.

Curiosity

Curiosity is a key reason that Intuit, maker of QuickBooks and TurboTax, has been able to disrupt itself and continue to grow over its 34-year history while other personal-software companies have disappeared.

Early in the company's history, when it only made personal-finance software, employees noticed that half of consumers were using the product at their offices. At first, Intuit assumed people were doing their home accounting at the office. Finally, curiosity broke through, and further investigation revealed that the customers were using the product to run small businesses. This observation about consumer behavior led to a small-business product that now has 80 percent market share and constitutes half of Intuit's revenue.

For Intuit, curiosity means seeing through the customer's eyes, rather than through the company's eyes. A recent profile in *Fortune* said that Intuit conducts 10,000 hours of home visits each year.[1] Employees are trained not to ask questions during these visits, but instead just to observe how people use Intuit's products. Questions inevitably betray the hidden biases of the questioner, while observation of actual behavior can get closer to the truth.

Receptivity

Ford's new CEO, Jim Hackett, is another believer in putting a deep customer understanding at the center of business and design decisions. "Investing now in the understanding of use is the gift that will keep on giving," Hackett said in an October 2017 presentation to investors.

Hackett demonstrates serious receptivity to how changing consumer behavior, along with autonomous and electric vehicle technology, could radically change the role of Ford.

Ford's new vision statement shows this receptivity. It begins by stating that "freedom of movement drives human progress," linking that belief first to creating "great cars and trucks" and now to becoming "the world's most trusted mobility company, designing smart vehicles for a smart world."

Hackett recognizes something he calls the "perversity law," which means that "to stay competitive, businesses often have to give up the things that made them great in the first place," according to a piece in *The New York Times Magazine*.[2] Ford is not yet giving up on cars and trucks, or on its design and manufacturing expertise. However, it sees a future in which "there are many more choices for where we play and how we win," according to Hackett's investor presentation, including such heady ideas as "fully autonomous SAE Level 4 capable vehicles" and a "crowd-sourced dynamically routed shuttle service."

Fearlessness

Curious about consumer needs and new technology, and receptive to their profound implications, leading companies are fearless about acting on those implications.

Intuit recently become an open platform that encouraged collaboration with outside app developers, including competitors. Although this radical change had the potential to draw business away from Intuit, the company's leaders believed that this counter-intuitive move placed Intuit in the contemporary software ecosystem, providing more users with more options, and strengthening customer loyalty.

On a much larger scale, Ford is making big investments to position the company in many different roles: creating the software for self-driving cars that may or may not be manufactured by Ford, owning a transportation platform, and designing and manufacturing its own electric, autonomous vehicles. Ford has invested more than $4 billion in this effort, much of that in acquisition of startup companies. "Fearless" is a 114-year-old company relying on a one-year-old startup to develop the software for a self-driving car that could make or break the company's future.

Fresh Eyes for Healthcare

As new competitors from startups to behemoths train their eyes on the $3 trillion healthcare industry, hospital and health system executives are challenged—like Intuit and Ford—to hone their curiosity, receptivity, and fearlessness.

Curiosity. Healthcare relies largely on surveys and selected utilization data to understand how consumers use their services. However, these tools present a view that is framed by the legacy business model. Gene Woods, President and CEO of Carolinas HealthCare System, recently noted that nine out of 10 patient encounters at the system take place outside its walls.[3] These could be visits to the website, phone calls, emails, virtual visits, community events. Woods asks, "What do we know about these encounters? Who and where are they? How do people access us and what do they want? We're asking these questions, and this mindset is causing us to shift our investment portfolio." This is the kind of curiosity health systems need to have. We need to develop methods to see more directly into consumer behavior in relationship to individuals' health needs—to see through the consumers' eyes rather than through our legacy viewpoint.

Receptivity. We need to be open to new roles for our organizations, roles that may result in very different kinds of organizations in the future. Just as CVS Health recast itself from a pharmacy chain to a healthcare company, hospitals and health systems need to consider whether their role is limited to caring for patients or is something broader, given the breadth of consumers' health and healthcare experiences. Several years ago, Intermountain Healthcare changed its mission to "Helping people live the healthiest lives possible." The mission is receptive to the many ways an organization can encourage health, and it presents health as something open to different definitions by different participants.

Fearlessness. Any change in role flies in the face of the status quo, involves uncertainty about outcomes, and in many disruptive scenarios could result in reduced revenue in the short term as organizations prepare for the long term. All of these factors are likely to make staff members, executives, and board members anything from uncomfortable to outright resistant. However, based on a strong financial plan, organizations need to start placing bets on new roles and capabilities. UPMC in Pennsylvania recently invested $2 billion in three specialty "digital hospitals of the future," which will be designed in collaboration with Microsoft. UPMC's announcement says that these hospitals will "radically change healthcare as we know it."[4]

Savoring the Surprise

Imagine Amazon CEO Jeff Bezos sitting in his office one day when an employee came in and said, "We have a ton of server capacity, and we're really good at managing it. Why don't we start selling cloud services?"

Instead of replying, "We're an online retailer, not a cloud services company," Bezos launched a new line of business that today earns almost $10 billion per year and constitutes more than half of Amazon's annual operating income.[5]

Bezos was doing what Intuit executives call "savoring the surprise." Instead of questioning or resisting the information, instead of trying to protect the status quo, he and other successful executives welcome new insights and eagerly explore their implications for the business, even if that means radical change. It is a crucial part of the regular self-disruption that makes for an effective business in the Internet economy.

Looking at healthcare through fresh eyes will yield many surprises for hospital executives—surprises about the way consumers interact with the broader healthcare system, and what changes in the patient experience would create meaningful engagement. Being open to these changes, and acting fearlessly to make them happen, are the keys to disrupting your own organization before others do that job for you.

References

1 Colvin, G.: "How Intuit Reinvents Itself." *Fortune*, Oct. 20, 2017.

2 Roose, K." "Can Ford Turn Itself into a Tech Company?." *The New York Times Magazine*, Nov. 9, 2017.

3 Skogsbergh, J., Woods, E.: "Reorienting Healthcare." Kaufman Hall, Nov. 14, 2018.

4 "UPMC Announces $2B Investment to Build 3 Digitally Based Specialty Hospitals Backed by World-Leading Innovative, Translational Science." UPMC, Nov. 3, 2017.

5 Wingfield, N.: "Amazon's Cloud Business Lifts Its Profit to a Record." *The New York Times*, Apr. 28, 2016.

Creating the Future

"Companies never choose to die, and yet many by not evolving are enabling that kind of fate."[1]

That was the message this month from Jim Hackett, new CEO of Ford, to investors nervous that the company was moving too slowly into the future of mobility—a future expected to be dominated by electric vehicles, self-driving vehicles, and new attitudes toward vehicle ownership.

Ford had been changing. Alan Mulally, Ford's CEO from 2006 to 2014, engineered a turnaround after the nation's financial crisis by scrubbing Ford's portfolio of brands, reducing the number of plants, and cutting staff.[2] Ford's next CEO, Mark Fields, created the Ford Smart Mobility subsidiary to develop the software and tech services needed for self-driving cars,[3] and pledged that Ford would mass-market a self-driving car for ride-sharing by 2021.[4]

Ford may have been changing, but by the measure of the Internet economy, Ford wasn't changing fast enough. "The world's impression of Ford is that they are behind on a lot of these technologies," said one analyst,[5] an attitude reflected in a 40 percent drop in Ford's stock price since 2014.[6] In his May announcement that Fields would be replaced, Ford Chairman William C. Ford said, "Look at the pace of change and the competitors coming into our space, and we need to match or beat that."[7] The competitors he had in mind were not other traditional automakers—although they, too, are investing in self-driving and electric cars—but companies like Tesla, Google, Apple, and Uber.

The CEO's Job in the Internet Economy

Hackett's message applies to companies in any industry facing disruption by the Internet economy. Blockbuster didn't choose to die, but it didn't move aggressively enough to avoid the tsunami of streaming video. Borders didn't choose to die, but it didn't move aggressively enough into online fulfillment and e-books.

In hindsight, those conclusions are clear. However, in the Internet economy, the challenge for virtually any company is to prepare for a future that lacks the clarity offered by hindsight.

A disruptive future looms large in healthcare. UnitedHealth, number 6 on the Fortune 500, is rapidly growing its urgent care, surgery center, and analytics presence through the Optum subsidiary. CVS, number 7 on the Fortune 500, offers routine primary care, is moving into chronic care, and has a MinuteClinic within 10 miles of home for half of all Americans.[8] And recently we learned that Apple, number 3 on the Fortune 500 and with a market cap of $800 billion, was in negotiations to buy a medical-clinic network.[9] At the same time, emerging technology like telehealth, precision medicine, and artificial intelligence all hold the promise to fundamentally shift the economics and delivery of healthcare.

Hackett's challenge at Ford is basically the same challenge faced by healthcare executives across the country: to envision the future, identify the organization's new role, and move aggressively to organize and execute around that vision.

Envision the Future

In an environment in which the iPhone changed the world in 10 years, envisioning the future requires imagination and vigilant attention to new technology, business dynamics, and consumer preferences.

Five years ago, it would have been hard to predict that the market valuation of an electric car maker, Tesla, would surpass that of Ford and GE,[10] and that annual investment in auto-tech companies would be more than $1 billion.[11] Ford is envisioning a future in which electricity is the predominant means of propulsion, vehicles communicate with their environment and with each other, and different types of smart vehicles and resources enable a wide variety of mobility from bicycling to shuttle services.

In healthcare, five years ago it would have been hard to predict that more than half of Kaiser Permanente's patient-physician encounters would be virtual,[12] that CVS would have had more than 30 million patient visits,[13] and that $750 million would be invested in one year in healthcare-related artificial-intelligence startups.[14] Yet healthcare executives will need to place some bets on how new technology, competition, and consumer expectations will transform the industry.

Identify the Organization's New Role

Hackett calls identifying a future role a "winning aspiration." In addition to manufacturing autonomous electrical vehicles, Ford has identified potential roles in fleet management, mobility apps, shuttle services, ride-hailing services, medical transportation, and digital services. Many of these roles would require that Ford look beyond the traditional go-it-alone approach and develop multiple partnerships for various specialized capabilities. These options also require that Ford have a radically different organizational and operating structure, and a different pool of intellectual capital. Perhaps most daunting, none of these options has a proven revenue model.

Legacy healthcare organizations face equally tough questions when trying to determine their future role: They must articulate a unique value proposition that builds on their strengths and positions them for the future—for example, specializing in treatment of highly complex cases, convenience and patient experience, or the best care at the lowest cost. They need to consider new kinds of services outside the traditional inpatient core. And they need to consider the revenue and cost implications of these options.

Organize and Execute Around that Vision

Corporate "fitness" is the term that Hackett uses to describe the job of organizing and executing on the company's future role. For Ford, "fitness" includes:

- **Attacking costs.** At Ford, costs have grown at the same pace as revenue. Ford plans to bend the cost curve with a $14 billion reduction in engineering and material costs over five years

- **Optimizing its portfolio.** Ford will reallocate $7 billion of capital from cars to SUVs and trucks, and redeploy 32 percent of its capital spending from internal combustion to electrification

- **Redesigning business operations.** Ford wants to reduce its new-vehicle development time and design a "factory of the future" with a smaller footprint and faster logistics

- **Focusing on deep learning.** Ford will invest in understanding people's expectations for mobility, and in new ways that vehicles can interact with people, each other, and the environment

- **Entering into partnerships.** Ford will escalate partnerships that deliver solutions more rapidly than Ford could accomplish on its own

- **Developing the right culture.** Ford's goals are to focus the workforce on "human-centered mobility solutions" and to ensure that teams are empowered, work together effectively, and have a sense of urgency

These elements of corporate fitness readily translate into healthcare, where organizations need to fundamentally rework their cost structures, service portfolios, care models, analytics, partnerships, and cultures for a new environment. Each of these is a formidable task requiring clarity of purpose, a roadmap with metrics and timelines, and accountability.

A Sense of Urgency

Ford's previous CEO was replaced after three years. He wasn't fired for inaction or for not understanding the elements of change, but for not moving quickly and aggressively enough to be competitive in the Internet environment. In contrast, Hackett told investors, "The mandate here is that Ford must compete."

In healthcare or in the automotive industry, the changes needed to compete in the Internet economy are enormous. They require vision and creativity. They require new levels of cash flow, access to capital, and intellectual capital. They require new analytics, structures, processes, and behaviors. And they require a culture that transcends political sensitivities and the status quo with an appetite for innovation.

The bigger the task, the sooner it must start, especially in a fast-changing environment. In that spirit, Hackett's words to Ford's investors would serve well for healthcare executives:

"I get up every day feeling like time can be wasted here if we don't get moving."

References

1 Naughton, K.: "Ford to Slash $14 Billion in Costs Under New CEO." *Bloomberg*, Oct. 3, 2017.

2 Jurnecka, R.: "Mulally's Testimony Emphasizes Ford's Goal of Fuel Efficiency, Cost Cutting." *MotorTrend*, Dec. 4, 2008.

3 Griffith, E., "Who Will Build the Next Great Car Company?" *Fortune*, Jun. 23, 2016.

4 Sage, A., Lienert, P.: "Ford Plans Self-Driving Car for Ride Share Fleets in 2021." *Reuters*, Aug. 16, 2016.

5 Naughton, K.: "Ford to Slash $14 Billion in Costs Under New CEO." *Bloomberg*, Oct. 3, 2017.

6 Priddle, A.: "Mark Fields Out as Ford CEO; Replaced by Jim Hackett." *MotorTrend*, May 22, 2017.

7 Vlasic, B.: "Ford Installs a New C.E.O." *The New York Times*, May 22, 2017.

8 Commins, J.: "CVS Health Posts Strong Retail, Omnicare Outlook." *HealthLeaders*, Feb. 10, 2016.

9 Farr, C. "Apple explored buying a medical-clinic start-up as part of a bigger push into health care." CNBC, Oct. 21, 2017.

10 "Tesla Hits a New Milestone, Passing G.M. in Valuation." *The New York Times*, Apr. 10, 2017.

11 Newcomb, D.: "Car Tech Startup Investment Exceeds $1 Billion In 2016." *Forbes*, Jan. 27, 2017.

12 Barkholz, D.: "Kaiser Permanente Chief Says Members are Flocking to Virtual Visits." *Modern Healthcare*, Apr. 21, 2017.

13 "CVS MinuteClinic Announces the Cure for the Common Wait as it Unveils a Digital Tool Allowing Patients to Hold a Place in Line." *PRNewswire*, May 26, 2016.

14 "The State of Artificial Intelligence." *CB Insights*, Apr. 11, 2017.

The Second Response to Disruption

OCTOBER 12, 2017

W hen any disruptive force appears to threaten the physical wellbeing of patients—or the financial wellbeing of hospitals and physicians—the understandable first response is to push back. Particularly with respect to patient health, this initial response is necessary and important. However, when going up against major industry change, a *second* response may have the longer-term effect.

The Disruptive Force

Anthem Blue Cross recently instituted two new policies in many of the states it serves.[1] One eliminates payment for non-emergency visits to the hospital emergency department. The other declines to pay for outpatient MRIs and CT scans performed in hospitals, unless Anthem deems that setting medically necessary.

These are among the most aggressive policies we have seen yet to steer patients away from high-cost hospital services and toward lower cost, non-traditional alternatives such as retail clinics, urgent care clinics, and freestanding diagnostic chains.

The First Response

Provider representatives have been quick to point out the potential hardships for patients, providers, and communities, and the potential conflict with current law.

Quality and patient protection. "Economically motivated steerage of patients compromises the physician-patient relationship and undercuts integrated health care efforts," said the American College of Radiology in a statement about Anthem's new imaging payment policy.[2] In a letter to Anthem about its policy to not pay for non-emergency care in a hospital emergency department, the American Medical Association said, "The impact of this policy is that very ill and vulnerable patients will not seek needed emergency medical care while, bluntly, their conditions worsen or they die."[3]

Deficits among the alternative providers. The American College of Radiology "is concerned that Anthem's policy will force patients to locate an ever-declining number of freestanding imaging centers and/or physician's offices to access imaging services" and that "such facilities may not be immediately prepared to care for an influx of patients…"

Law and regulation. The American College of Emergency Physicians said that Anthem's emergency department payment policy "is a clear violation of the national prudent layperson standard, which is codified in federal law."[4] That standard "requires that insurance coverage is based on a patient's symptoms and not their final diagnosis."

Financial hardship for hospitals and their communities. The American College of Radiology said that "Forcing all advanced imaging out of hospital outpatient departments may prompt many of these facilities to cut back on standard imaging…or close altogether. This may be particularly true in areas where hospitals care for many indigent patients."

The Second Response

As I described in a recent blog post, Anthem's new rules are a case of disruption straight out of the Clay Christensen playbook: An innovative entity offers a product or service in a more convenient way and at a lower price, drawing volume away from the legacy provider. The wrinkle in healthcare is that, historically, the entity paying for the service has been different from the one using the service. However, insurance plans increasingly are designed to align consumers and payers around low prices, and a high level of convenience is designed to further move traffic toward these disruptive innovators.

For health plans, the change is clearly designed to lower costs. For hospitals, the likely result is a shift in volume and revenue away from hospitals and toward new locations of care.

After hospitals' initial response on immediate issues of patient safety, the question is what the second response should be.

The key is not to limit the response to simply protecting the status quo. For example, when ESPN was first removed from the cable bundle, its so-called strategic response was to sue Verizon. When the taxi industry first felt the competition from Uber, it argued safety concerns and used existing regulations in an attempt to block Uber. What ESPN and the taxi industry did not do promptly enough was to address the underlying causes of disruption and the fast-changing competitive environment.

In regard to payers resisting hospitals prices, the underlying causes are stark and complex. Hospital prices are 235 percent of freestanding provider prices for CT scans and 170 percent of freestanding provider prices for MRIs. An emergency department visit costs about four times a visit to an urgent care clinic.[5] At a time when healthcare costs are 18 percent of the nation's GDP[6] and 43 percent of adults have trouble affording their deductible, this kind of price variation makes hospitals highly vulnerable to lower prices and other ways of delivering care.

At the same time, consumers seeking routine services are unlikely to be open to an argument about differences in quality, especially when at least one outpatient radiology chain has scans read by Cleveland Clinic physicians.[7] And arguments about patient convenience at hospitals are unlikely to sway consumers when less than half of hospitals and health systems have extended hours for diagnostic services.[8]

In a disruptive environment, economics and consumer preference *always* prevail. The *second* response to disruption, therefore, needs to promptly and aggressively address the vulnerabilities of price and consumer experience that give rise to disruption.

Hospitals and health systems need to be much more serious about cost reduction through strategies such as repurposing low-performing facilities or eliminating unnecessary service duplication. They need to get deep information about consumer demographics, health status, usage patterns, expectations, and attitudes. They need to infuse this consumer understanding into all aspects of strategic and operational planning, including service design. They need to develop a comprehensive pricing strategy that takes into account market prices and likely effect on utilization of pricing changes. And they need to explore partnerships that may enhance patient access and experience.

The first response to disruption should always respect the safety of patients. The second response should focus on the future of the organization. Time spent protecting the status quo takes attention from a far more strategic objective: eliminating the vulnerabilities that invite disruption.

References

1   Livingston, S.: "Anthem's New Outpatient Imaging Policy Likely to Hit Hospitals' Bottom Line."
    Modern Healthcare, Aug. 26, 2017.

2   Walter, M.: "ACR: Anthem's New Outpatient Imaging Policy is 'Arbitrary,' 'Unwise.'" *Radiology Business*,
    Aug. 29, 2017.

3   Robeznieks, A.: "Physicians protest harmful Anthem emergency care coverage policy." American
    Medical Association, Aug. 7, 2017.

4   "Emergency Physicians: Anthem Blue Cross Blue Shield Policy Violates Federal Law." American College
    of Emergency Physicians, May 16, 2017.

5   Findlay, S.: "When You Should Go to an Urgent Care or Walk-in Health Clinic." *Consumer Reports*,
    May 4, 2018.

6   *National Health Expenditures 2017 Highlights*. Centers for Medicare & Medicaid Services, 2017.

7   Kaufman, K.: "A Clear and Present Disruption." Kaufman Hall, May 10, 2016.

8   *2017 State of Consumerism in Healthcare*, Kaufman Hall & Associates, 2017.

Amazon's Big Picture

JULY 16, 2017

Amazon CEO Jeff Bezos paints on a big canvas. The canvas is so big that it is nearly impossible to step back far enough to appreciate the full picture. The fact that the picture is getting larger and being embellished every day makes it even more difficult to grasp its dimension and interconnections.

There is little doubt that Bezos is the smartest businessperson in the country right now, and I doubt that anyone fully perceives Amazon's strategy. However, Amazon's recently announced agreement to acquire Whole Foods for $14 billion is a useful lens to view some key elements of that strategy—and how it differentiates Amazon.

Amazon Is Bringing the Old Economy into the New Economy

Google and Facebook are intent on creating the tools, interactions, and experiences of the Internet economy, and on monetizing that economy. In contrast, Amazon is intent on using the tools of the Internet economy to change the direction and competitive dynamics of the post-industrial economy.

For Amazon, integrating the new and old economies creates a whole that is greater than the sum of its parts. Amazon has transformed the shopping experience with sophisticated algorithms, artificial intelligence, and high-tech fulfillment. Amazon has transformed the reading experience with e-books, streaming audiobooks, and voice-activated custom audio news. Bezos is even beginning to transform the business of newspaper publishing with his ownership of the *Washington Post*. By transforming these experiences, Amazon takes the old economy and creates new consumer demand and a new business model.

The acquisition of Whole Foods is perhaps the best example of this strategy. Grocery shopping is the ultimate example of the old economy. Food trails only housing and transportation as a percentage of consumer spending, and consumer spending on groceries is roughly equal to consumer spending on healthcare, according to the Bureau of Labor Statistics.[1] Grocery shopping is an in-person experience that has been updated only modestly over the years. Despite widespread awareness of the inconveniences of grocery shopping—parking, finding items, waiting in checkout lines—companies like Walmart, Peapod, and Amazon itself have yet to transform grocery shopping into an Internet-era experience. Whole Foods provides Amazon with a large sandbox to figure out how to make that transformation. In the process, Amazon will create even more loyal customers by owning another major segment of consumer spending.

Amazon Does Not Care About Walmart

It is tempting to assess Amazon's acquisition of Whole Foods in terms of the effect on so-called competitors, particularly Walmart, which has been striving to integrate in-person and on-line shopping. However, Amazon's acquisition of Whole Foods is part of a very different strategy than trying to surpass Walmart or any other competitor. Amazon's measure of success will not be its profit as a grocery seller, but its ability to create a transcendent consumer experience. Amazon has unmatched experience, infrastructure, creativity, and capital to make that happen. Expect Amazon to figure out how to speak your order to Alexa and get fresh items delivered quickly, use a GPS to lead you to any item you want at the Whole Foods store, use a smartphone scan as a substitute for a checkout line, and even more radical ideas still known only to Amazon.

Even that transformation is not an end in itself for Amazon. Selling groceries is another component of Amazon's larger bid for broad-based essentiality. It is one more way to provide Amazon more traffic, more data, and more ways to be integral to the lives of more people.

For Amazon, Process Is as Important as Outcomes

Bezos once said in a letter to shareholders, "I believe we are the best place in the world to fail."[2]

Amazon's failures have not been small. The Amazon Fire phone cost the company hundreds of millions of dollars, but Bezos said, "We're working on much bigger failures...some of them are going to make the Fire Phone look like a tiny little blip."

For Amazon, failure is a necessary part of experimentation. If you're not failing, you're not experimenting enough. Amazon sees Whole Foods as a part of the unending process of experimentation—in this case, an experiment that will allow the company to learn about the grocery business and about commerce in a bricks-and-mortar setting, where more than 90 percent of consumer spending still takes place. Buying Whole Foods will help Amazon master the in-person retail experience and attach that retail experience to the Internet economy, and in the process create a brand new retail experience.

Amazon's Dominance Is Structural

The foundation that allows Amazon to have such a farsighted business strategy is its structural dominance.[3] That dominance has many ingredients. One is the extraordinary loyalty and spending generated by its Prime program. Estimates suggest that Amazon Prime has

65 million members,[4] and they spend 4.6 times the amount of non-Prime Amazon shoppers.[5] Another foundation of Amazon's dominance is its enormous scale as a retailer, offering almost 400 million items[6] to 183 million average monthly site visitors.[7]

Finally, by developing its business-to-business services, primarily cloud storage and sales fulfillment—Amazon has become essential not just to consumers, but also to other businesses, including Amazon's competitors. A recent Wall Street Journal headline says it all: "Walmart to Vendors: Get Off Amazon's Cloud."[8]

Amazon's big picture is to be everywhere. Through a complex integration of sales, service, experience, and infrastructure, Amazon is well on its way to embedding itself throughout every big and little corner of the economy. That is not just a big picture, but perhaps the very biggest business picture. Amazon's $14 billion purchase of Whole Foods is just the latest element in Amazon's grand design to remake the commercial superstructure of America.

References

1 *Consumer Expenditures—2022*, Bureau of Labor Statistics, Sept. 8, 2023.

2 Kim, E.: "How Amazon CEO Jeff Bezos has inspired people to change the way they think about failure." *Business Insider*, May 28, 2016.

3 Khan, L.M.: "Amazon's Antitrust Paradox." *The Yale Law Journal*, Jan. 2017.

4 Gustafson, K.: "Amazon hints at one of Its Best-Kept Secrets: How Many Prime Members it Has." CNBC, Feb. 17, 2017.

5 Kim, E.: "Amazon Just Made Thousands of Books Free for Its Prime Members — Here's a Simple Reason Why." *Business Insider*, Oct. 6, 2016.

6 "How Many Products Are Sold on Amazon.com – January 2017 Report." *ScrapeHero*, Jan. 5, 2017.

7 "Leading e-Commerce Websites in the United States as of June 2021, Based on Number of Monthly Visits." Statista, Jun. 2021.

8 Greene, J., Stevens, L.: "Wal-Mart to Vendors: Get Off Amazon's Cloud." *The Wall Street Journal*, Jun. 21, 2017.

Power to the Patients

JUNE 14, 2016

For decades, we've talked about doing a better job of involving patients in their healthcare decisions and treatment. As important as that goal is, it's only an incremental step away from the traditional roles of the controlling provider and the dependent patient. And incremental steps aren't enough for consumers in the Internet economy.

The Internet has provided rocket fuel for people to take control away from traditional structures. Just ask record companies, taxi companies, or newspapers. Progress has been slower in healthcare, with its entrenched traditions, complexities, and regulations. However, we are starting to see significant examples of people using the Internet and related technology to completely bypass physicians and legacy healthcare systems.

A great example is the Nightscout Project, described in a recent *JAMA* article.[1] The parents of a 4-year-old boy with type 1 diabetes found that they could not access readings from their son's regular glucose monitor while he was in school. The boy's father, a software programmer, created a program to bring the glucose readings from the device into the cloud, where the parents could access them from anywhere via their smartphones.

A Tweet about his achievement led to inquiries from caregivers and patients with technical expertise, and ultimately to the Nightscout Project online collaborative. The group developed mobile solutions for diabetes monitoring, including smartphone apps that provide alerts for abnormal glucose levels, and a web application and wearable device to display glucose readings. The project has a Facebook group of more than 15,000 members in the United States and 4,000 members in other countries, and a website where anyone can download the open code and set up their own system.

Here is a breakthrough that is developed by a parent, makes use of wearable and cloud technology, and is shared through social media. No healthcare professionals are involved.

This is not an isolated example. A 15-year-old invented a sensor that alerts his family via smartphone when his grandfather, who has Alzheimer's and is prone to wandering, gets out of bed at night.[2] His project was recognized at the Google Science Fair and spawned a popular Ted Talk. Start-up companies are also helping people bypass the traditional health system. Wellness FX offers direct-to-consumer blood tests by connecting patients with local labs, delivering easy-to-understand results to personal accounts on the website, and offering a virtual physician consultation about the results.[3] Any Lab Test Now, which has more than 150 locations, provides direct consumer access to clinical lab tests, including providing a doctor's order for patients who do not have one; results go to the consumer rather than to the physician.[4]

A handful of forward-looking legacy health systems have taken steps toward giving more power to patients. For example, Kaiser Permanente Northwest has allowed women to self-refer for mammograms since 1991.[5] However, start-ups are clearly taking the lead, and funders see great promise, with venture-capital investment in on-demand healthcare companies estimated to reach more than $1 billion by 2017.[6]

The movement toward patient-powered healthcare is causing plenty of consternation from legacy entities about lack of care coordination and regulatory compliance, the possible increase in utilization and therefore costs, and the need for physician oversight. These concerns may be valid, but they do not change the basic fact: In the Internet economy, patients can and will take control of their healthcare. Legacy healthcare entities cannot stop this trend any more than newspaper publishers can convince people to put down their smartphones.

Today, people don't have to stand in the rain fruitlessly searching for a taxi. They don't have to wait for the next day's newspaper to get the news. And increasingly they don't have to wait for a traditional provider to grant permission to access care or health information. In the Internet economy, people no longer have to accept things they cannot change; instead, they change things they cannot accept. That same attitude needs to become a core belief for traditional healthcare providers.

References

1   Lee, J.M., Hirschfeld, E., Wedding, J.: "A Patient-Designed Do-It-Yourself Mobile Technology System for Diabetes." *Journal of the American Medical Association*, 315(14), April 12, 2016.

2   Singal, J.: "A 15-Year-Old Came Up with a Really Smart Invention for Keeping Alzheimer's Patients Safe." *New York Magazine*, Sept. 19, 2014.

3   "How It Works." WellnessFX.

4   "About Us." AnyLabTestNow.

5   Moiel, D., Thompson, J.: "Early Detection of Breast Cancer Using a Self-Referral Mammography Process: The Kaiser Permanente Northwest 20-Year History." *The Permanente Journal* 18(1), Winter 2014.

6   Japsen, B.: "Health On-Demand Attracts $1B in Investments." *Forbes,* Feb. 2, 2016.

Talent

Rethinking Building High-Performing Professional Teams

APRIL 10, 2024

With Robert Fromberg, Senior Vice President, Kaufman Hall

In the early evening of Wednesday, June 5, 1974, in the visiting clubhouse of Tiger Stadium in Detroit, Oakland A's outfielders Reggie Jackson and Billy North got into not one but two fistfights. During the second of the two battles, Jackson injured his shoulder when North threw Jackson into a metal dressing stall. Trying to break up the second fight, Catcher Ray Fosse separated a cervical disk that required surgery. According to the contemporaneous account by the Associated Press, Jackson said that he had been on bad terms with North for a month after accusing North of not hustling. In later years, North admitted to relentlessly baiting Jackson leading to the clubhouse fight.

This was by no means the only conflict on the A's team that season. Players feuded with manager Alvin Dark, with third baseman Sal Bando saying Dark "couldn't manage a meat market." Players and the manager feuded with owner Charlie Finley. In the clubhouse the day before the opening of the 1974 World Series, pitcher Rollie Fingers threw a laundry cart at fellow pitcher Blue Moon Odom. We won't repeat the remark of Odom's that precipitated the attack.

The legendary conflict within the Oakland A's during the early 1970s did not prevent the team's success. Known as the Swingin' A's, the team won the World Series in 1972, 1973, and 1974, and won the American League West Division title five years in a row. It is even fair to ask whether the tendency toward conflict might have contributed to a spirit that fueled the team's success.

The story of the 1970s Oakland A's illustrates the complicated and important relationship between *capability* and *compatibility* in assessing individual and organizational professional effectiveness.

In the current environment, it is extremely hard to build and retain effective professional teams. Doing so requires a theoretical platform that helps leaders better understand what they are trying to accomplish and how to go about it. One framework for this assessment involves the relationship between two important curves: one that measures capability and the other that measures compatibility. What the Oakland A's shows us about this relationship is that the desired points on these curves are by no means obvious.

Defining Capability and Compatibility

We have entered an age in which organizational success is closely tied to the organizational IQ of the professional team that you've accumulated. Over the past 30 or 40 years, the organizations that have had the greatest success are the smartest. Amazon, Microsoft, Apple, Meta, and Google are among the most obvious examples. These were smart organizations to start with. They came up with incredibly smart ideas. They were smart about executing. And then as they created a culture of smart, they continued to hire smarter and smarter people.

When you interview a candidate, you run through a series of questions about their capability, their smartness. How much do they know about the job that they're being asked to do? How much experience do they have in doing that job? What is their track record of success? There's no doubt that when you interview different people for the same role, those people fall on very different places on the curve in those characteristics. Some people pop right out. They clearly are very smart. They clearly have a track record of success in that type of role.

Evaluating compatibility is perhaps more complex and in many cases more subjective. In business, compatibility can be seen as the extent to which a person works collaboratively within a team. At the highly compatible part of the curve would be people who thrive working with others, make everyone feel involved, and generate a solid outcome for their group. Moving toward the other end of the curve would be people who prefer to go their own way rather than to communicate and collaborate, and on the furthest point on the low end of this curve are those who actively and routinely create friction and conflict within the organization or otherwise make the lives of their colleagues more difficult, ultimately hurting the work product and perhaps even the success of the organization.

Applying the Capability/Compatibility Framework

On the face of it, applying this framework would seem straight-forward. The relationship of capability and compatibility lends itself to a standard four-box chart, on which the upper right box is high capability and high compatibility, and the lower left box is low capability and low compatibility. Presumably, an organization would try to recruit and retain people in the upper right box and avoid people in the lower left box.

Unfortunately, the analysis is not that simple. It depends on the precise capabilities and the extent to which an organization at a particular point in its history may be willing to tolerate incompatibility to get a certain type of capability, the extent to which an individual's capability level overcomes a deficit of compatibility and how that may change over time for that individual, and the organization's culture and goals.

Consider Apple, certainly one of the two or three most successful organizations in the world over the previous several decades. Steve Jobs was Apple's catalyst because his position on the capability curve was one of the highest in business history. However, he was legendarily low on the compatibility curve. In the early days of Apple, the kind of creativity and innovation that Jobs demonstrated was so important that the company was more than willing to accept low compatibility.

Jobs' successor was Tim Cook. Cook brought his own type of very high capability, and he raised the compatibility factor significantly. Cook's calming influence was essential as Apple dealt with the extraordinary operating and competitive complexity of today's tech world.

Let's say an organization has historically valued very low annoyance and has been willing to sacrifice capability in order to have high compatibility. And let's say that historically this organization has been reasonably successful financially and operationally. However, perhaps then the competition picks up and the chief executive and board don't feel like the organization is doing as well as it ought to be doing. Then the organization has to reevaluate whether it doesn't have sufficient high-capability talent because the organization has historically overemphasized this high-compatibility point of view.

This can also change when the CEO changes. Sometimes when a new CEO comes in and there are wholesale changes in the C-Suite, one of two things has happened. In one scenario, the CEO looked out into the organization and said, "It looks to me like what was really valued in this organization culturally was high compatibility, but we don't have enough high capability, which is why I've been brought in because the organization isn't doing very well. So I have to change the human resource culture of the organization to value high capability more than we valued it before." In the other scenario, the CEO looked out into the organization and said, "Our lack of compatibility is disrupting the organization to the extent that we can't operate effectively, can't compete effectively, and can't fulfill our mission. Some of this disruption comes from really smart people, but the level of incompatibility is outweighing any benefit we might be getting from their level of capability."

Organizations are at different places at different times, and they need to be empathetic to these factors depending on where they are. There might be periods of time when you need to hire people who are really smart and do their best work alone. They're not collaborative and they're not cooperative, but they produce exactly the work and exactly the outcome that the organization needs at that moment. But flash forward three years, and that personality type may be much less effective within an organization that now has to execute in a way that needs people for whom the team sense is stronger.

Self-evaluation of Capability and Compatibility

Let's face it. None of us is as smart as we may want to be. And none of us avoids rubbing others the wrong way at times. Our related levels of capability and compatibility are how others judge us and are central to how we influence our organizations. And those levels change over time. As business and technology issues evolve, it takes a serious effort to maintain a high level of capability. And as cultures change in the workplace and society as a whole, we may find ourselves grappling with definitions of compatibility that are nothing like those we understood earlier in our careers.

Executive self-awareness is extremely important in our environment right now, while 20 or 30 years ago you might have been able to have a perfectly good business career without being self-aware. Whether you're looking for a new job, or whether you're in an existing situation, you are being assessed and you should be assessing yourself. Where is your capability curve, and what is your relationship at any given moment within the organization on the compatibility curve?

Assessing Collective Relationships

None of us wants the kind of open warfare that the Oakland A's experienced in the early 1970s, but we would all love those three World Series rings. We all understand that the level of volatility experienced by the A's is not sustainable, and although the A's had an incredible run of success, perhaps the team would have had a more gradual but longer slope toward success if it had a different level of tolerance for incompatibility. We each have our own answer to the question of what level of volatility is worth tolerating for what level of success over what time period.

Executives need to ask themselves what kind of relationships they need for their particular organization at a particular point in time. How do you recognize that your cultural human resource process may have crossed over? Perhaps you had the right balance of capability and compatibility for what you were before, but now you're not that anymore and you need a different combination. How do you recognize that? And then how do you deal with the changing factor that people are not the same people all the time? Did you hire somebody with a certain capability/compatibility relationship and then five years later find that the relationship has changed? All these curves add up to a collective relationship, and how does the CEO understand what collective relationship he or she needs at a given point in time? And how does each executive understand his or her own value over time and ensure that he or she is the leader the organization needs at each point in the organization's progression?

In the 120 years during which Major League Baseball teams have competed in the World Series, only two teams won three or more successive championships. One team was, not surprisingly, the New York Yankees. (The Yankees won four championships in a row from 1936 to 1939, five in a row from 1949 to 1953, and three in a row from 1998 to 2000.) The only other team was none other than the Swingin' Oakland A's of the early 1970s.

Given the extraordinarily, nearly unprecedented, run of success the A's achieved in those years, and given the truly unusual makeup of the team, we must ask ourselves a question that may challenge some of our long-held and perhaps even cherished beliefs as leaders.

Is it possible that the A's achieved their extraordinary success *because* the team tolerated a level of incompatibility that most teams—and most organizations of any kind—would never tolerate? Is it possible that the A's success was not in spite of the personal conflicts, but actually as a direct result of the team organizing itself around a group of players with incredible capabilities who also happened to be associated with an extraordinary level of incompatibility, and were able to successfully manage through the resulting discord?

We suggest that this question is worth serious reflection for leaders of any organization aspiring to a world-class level of success.

Vision and Talent

FEBRUARY 7, 2024

Most of you who regularly read this blog know that I am an inveterate reader. I will read whatever is at hand: newspapers, magazines, blogs, and books. I am always keeping an eye out for commentary and suggestions that are relevant to the leadership and management of America's most complex organizations and institutions. Over time, I have learned to read carefully since an "article" that is seemingly about one thing might actually be making an entirely different point or an unexpected series of observations.

This happened recently when I came across an article in *The Athletic* written by David Lombardi.[1] The article was entitled "How a Stanford Professor Helped Lay the Foundation for this 49ers Era" (*The Athletic* is a daily sports paper and the San Francisco 49ers are a professional football team). Lombardi's article was about the rise of the 49ers from mediocrity in 2017 to a consistent Super Bowl contender: they appear again in this year's Super Bowl. At first glance this was sports reporting. But with a more careful read, it turned out this article was actually a business strategy piece masquerading as an article about professional sports.

The article followed the managerial trail of John Lynch—the 49ers' new general manager in 2017—as he considered how to bring the 49ers back to their former glory as five-time Super Bowl champions.

Lynch's first recognition was a macro-business observation and not exclusively a sports observation. And that perception was that talent is the characteristic that every organization (sports or otherwise) needs in order to generate consistent year-to-year success. Whether you're a football team, a bank, a software company, or a hospital provider, you can only succeed in this hyper-competitive economic era through the acquisition and retention of the very best talent.

Lynch wanted to establish a methodical approach at the 49ers for identifying the very best talent, but he quickly concluded that a random and undisciplined leadership approach would inevitably fall short. His first step forward toward a high-performing methodology was to hire a consultant (good move!!). The consultant he hired was Burke Robinson, a lecturer at Stanford University, who taught a class called "The Art and Science of Decision-Making." Robinson specialized in the development of vision statements for Silicon Valley start-ups.

As Robinson huddled with General Manager Lynch and Coach Kyle Shanahan, they put a priority on the development of a vision statement, but not the usual top-down vision statement that likely exists in your hospital organization. Instead, Lynch, Shanahan, and Robinson focused on developing a vision statement that would explicitly guide the selection and retention of talent that would return the 49ers to winning football. Coach Shanahan emphasized the importance of this process by noting that "culture is the people you surround yourself with." Over many years in both business and healthcare, I have read and heard many definitions of culture, but I had never before seen Shanahan's definition. In fact, that definition struck me as right, contemporary, and powerful.

From there the 49ers lead executives began building with Burke Robinson what I would call the talent vision statement. As Lombardi describes it, the process was complicated and involved much difficult discussion and back and forth between the key parties. Eventually the decision was made to organize the vision around two columns—on the left, what was called "49er talent," and on the right, what was called "49er spirit." The 2017 draft vision statement is illustrated below.

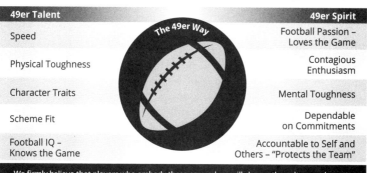

Source: *The Athletic,* courtesy Burke Robinson

What struck me immediately was how relevant this vision statement was to any complex organization or effort. Here it guides the drafting of football players, but just change the words and it proves to be a powerful vision to acquire and retain the very best talent in your hospital—both executive and clinical. Just as an example, try this "talent vision statement" on for size for your hospital or health system.

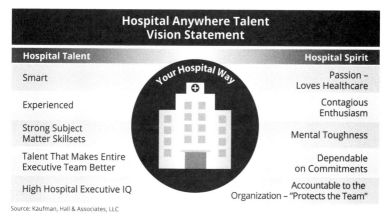

Source: Kaufman, Hall & Associates, LLC

As you can see, I have applied a list of characteristics to "Hospital Talent." I am sure many readers can and will generate their own list of critical talent characteristics. More interesting is how "49er Spirit" translates to the kind of spirit and intangibles that are required by any complex and competitive organization: day-to-day passion, enthusiasm and optimism, and mental toughness, which is absolutely required in today's hospital care environment. An effective team can only be built around talent that is dependable, and consistent competitive success demands total accountability in the best sense of that word.

When the 49er vision statement was completed, Lynch had that vision made into a large chart that was displayed prominently at 49er headquarters. The vision was also copied onto laminated cards and widely distributed within the 49er team and organization. Lynch concluded the interview with Lombardi by saying they wanted the team's vision "to be about who we really are. It's a beacon that reminds us who we are and what we are trying to be." As I said at the beginning of this blog, this excellent piece by David Lombardi is a business article masquerading as sports article. Read carefully: important leadership wisdom and guidance can be found in the most unexpected places.

References

1   Lombardi, D.: "How a Stanford Professor Helped Lay the Foundation for this 49ers Era." *The Athletic*, Jan. 17, 2024.

Comments on Current Management Issues in the Healthcare C-Suite: Management of Labor in Trying Financial Circumstances

JULY 28, 2023

With Erik Swanson, Senior Vice President, Kaufman Hall

Peter Drucker, the hall of fame management guru, once famously said that the hardest business organization to run in America was a hospital. If that comment was true so many years ago, imagine what Drucker would have to say about the difficulty of hospital management right now.

Hospital financial performance suffered significantly in 2022 and recovery during 2023 has been quite slow. This trend suggests the question, "What steps are hospital C-suites taking to recover pre-COVID financial stability?"

Erik Swanson manages all analyses for our monthly *Kaufman Hall Flash Report* and he and I speculated that an industry-wide hospital recovery could not be achieved without reductions in force across the hospital ecosystem. Some research on our part determined that no official organization tracks hospital layoffs over time but we wondered if we could use our *Flash Report* data to reach an informed conclusion.

What we were able to do was prepare three types of charts, as follows:

The first chart measures net employee percentage change by month. This chart shows whether overall hospital employment is increasing or decreasing over time and by how much.

The second chart attempts to establish the median turnover for hospitals over an annual period and then measure the deviation from that turnover rate. A greater deviation from what might be termed "normal turnover" suggests that an increasing number of hospitals are using reductions in force to more quickly reduce the cost of doing business.

The third chart shows average FTEs per occupied bed on a comparative basis looking at month-to-month and year-to-year statistics.

The first chart, Net Employee Percentage Change by Month, begins at January 1, 2018, and continues to March 1, 2023 (Figure 1). Overall additions to hospital employment remained generally positive through January 1, 2020. Overall hospital employment then went generally negative from March 2020 (the onset of COVID restrictions) to March 2022. The reductions in hospital employees during this period were likely the result of the "great resignation" during the worst of the COVID pandemic. But then, from July 2022 to March 2023, overall hospital employees demonstrated by the *Flash Report* dropped dramatically with an overall 2% decrease at the March 2023 date. This statistic suggests more than simply increased hospital turnover, but rather a formal layoff process initiated across many hospital organizations, along with aggressive management of contract labor.

The second chart demonstrates the deviation from expected turnover at levels of 2x, 3x, 4x, and 5x by number of hospitals (Figure 2). No matter which measure you examine, the deviation

Figure 1: Net Employee Percentage Change by Month

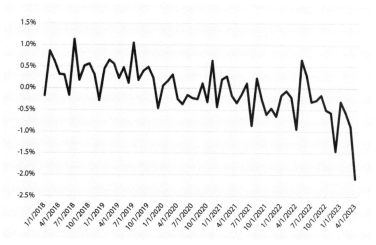

Figure 2: Number of Hospitals with Deviations from Expected Turnover at 2x, 3x, 4x, and 5x the Median

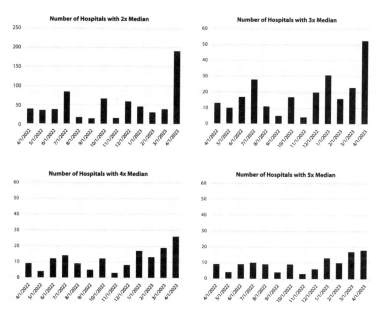

Figure 3: Median Change in FTEs per Adjusted Occupied Bed by Month

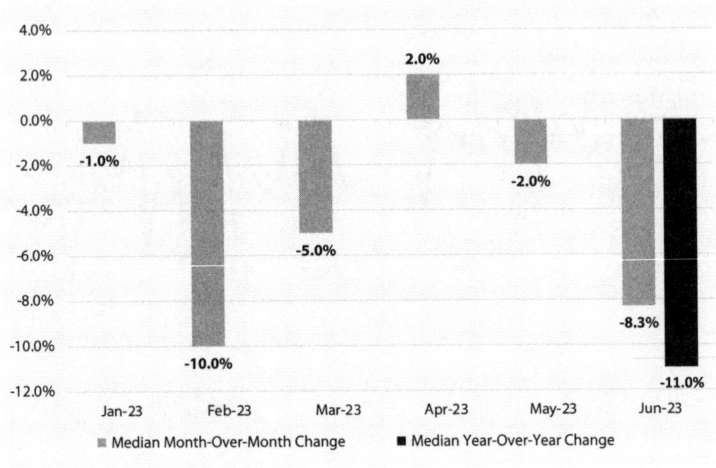

Source: Kaufman, Hall & Associates, LLC

of employees from expected turnover spiked significantly in April 2023 and even more so in May 2023. This again suggests the aggressive management of labor costs that likely could not occur without the intentional reduction of actual positions and/or the cost of these positions.

The last chart provides a remarkable set of observations (Figure 3). FTEs per adjusted occupied bed (AOB) declined by 8.3% between June 2023 and July 2023. The year-over-year variation for July 2023 was a decline of 11.01%. Our data further reveals that the FTE per AOB statistic has declined in five of the past six months on a month-over-month basis.

The conclusion here is that the return of the hospital industry to pre-COVID financial results has been no walk in the park. 2022 was, of course, a dismal financial year for the hospital industry. And while 2023 has shown improvement, the usual management steps to recovery have been only moderately effective. The data and analysis above demonstrate that C-suites across America are moving to stronger measures to assure the financial survivability and competitiveness of their organizations. There is no revenue solve here, or at least not in the current environment: costs must come down and they must come down materially. From the sense and the trend of the data it would seem that hospital executive teams get the joke.

The Workforce Challenge Is a Segmentation Challenge

DECEMBER 8, 2021

n my conversations with senior executives at healthcare organizations around the country, I find that leaders have three critical topics on their minds: workforce, workforce, and workforce. And no wonder.

Between May and September of this year, 20 million Americans voluntarily left their jobs, in what has been called The Great Resignation.[1] That number has risen each month, culminating—so far—with 4.4 million resignations in September, or 3% of the total workforce.

Over that five-month period, 2.6 million of those resignations came in what the Bureau of Labor Statistics calls the "healthcare and social assistance" category. Resignations in the healthcare sector increased 3.9% over the previous year, second only to the tech sector, according to a study published in the *Harvard Business Review*.[2] That study concluded that resignations were higher in fields where employees were most susceptible to burnout from "extreme increases in demand due to the pandemic."

As challenging as the resignation situation is, it is only one part of the workforce upheaval catalyzed by the pandemic.

One high-profile issue is work setting. A Gallup study found that 69% of workers were remote in May of 2020, during the thick of the pandemic, and that percentage has been hovering between 45% and 50% over the past year for all employees and around 69% for white-collar workers.[3]

Feelings about remote versus in-person work are very strong. On Wall Street, for example, Goldman Sachs CEO David Solomon said in February that working from home is "an aberration that we're going to correct as soon as possible."[4] Morgan Stanley CEO James Gorman said, "If you want to get paid New York rates, you work in New York." And JPMorgan Chase CEO Jamie Dimon said, "Oh, yes, people don't like commuting, but so what?" In contrast, Jefferies Financial Group CEO Richard Handler said, "Our people did not spend the day streaming movies, commiserating about the pain of life in isolation or hiding in any way from their obligations. They worked harder and more effectively than at any time in our firm's history."

The ability to work remotely has proven to be a huge factor not only in job satisfaction, but in willingness of people to continue at their current jobs. More than 90% of U.S. workers surveyed by Gallup said that they hope to continue working remotely to some degree after the pandemic.[5] Equally important, almost one-third of employees surveyed said they are "extremely likely to seek another job if their company eliminates remote work."

I would suggest an important way to tackle the highly charged and highly complex workforce problem is to view it as a matter of segmentation.

For example, not all workers have the luxury of working remotely. As of May 2021, less than one-quarter of healthcare providers and support staff were working remotely,[6] compared with three-quarters of workers in what the BLS calls "professional and related" occupations. The segmentation issue is, of course, much broader and deeper than remote work. An additional 1.4 million mothers with school-age children found themselves forced to leave the paid workforce during the pandemic, due to lack of in-person school and childcare, according to the U.S. Census Bureau.[7]

Social inequities that COVID laid bare were highly apparent in workforce effects.[8] At the outset of the pandemic, unemployment rates, which spiked for all workers, were significantly higher for Black men, Black women, and White women than they were for White men. Black workers who were able to maintain their employment were far less likely than White workers to have the luxury of doing their jobs remotely, because Black workers make up a disproportionate share of front-line workers, including in healthcare. As a result, Blacks have had greater exposure to the health risks of COVID in the workplace than have Whites.

Like its effects, any solution to the workforce problem needs to focus on segmentation.

In the world of human resources, the default setting—in no small part for valid compliance reasons—is to generally apply the same policies to workers across the board. However, the current workforce crisis has emphasized that any workforce, especially a healthcare workforce, has many subtly different segments of people and jobs, and each segment reacts differently to the social, economic, cultural, and working environment.

The job of human resources in large, diverse organization is inherently complex. And managing the immediate problems of turnover and workforce shortages has made that job immeasurably harder. Unfortunately, addressing the causes of the Great Resignation, with its multi-segment dimensions, will be harder still.

Healthcare organizations will have to identify the relevant worker segments. They will have to figure out what people in each segment need and value, and what makes a job attractive. For example, what do the women in your workforce want? What causes women in your area to take jobs, and what causes them to stay? What do you have to do related to compensation, childcare, flexibility of hours, education support, and paths to advancement?

What would a similar analysis show for environmental services workers? For food service workers? For nurses? For physicians?

With organizations already stretched thin, this sort of deep and sophisticated analysis will be extremely challenging, to say the least. Equally challenging will be deciding on and taking action.

Over-analysis is always a danger in large organizations, as is unwillingness to take bold action in areas as sensitive as workforce. If anything, healthcare organizations tend to be more cautious than other organizations, and for good reason, given the role they play in people's lives both as care providers and large employers.

However, one of the hallmarks of the COVID period has been rapid socioeconomic and cultural change. The Great Resignation has emerged quickly and is escalating. In the absence of rapid action, organizations run a risk of significant damage to their market positions and even their ability to carry out core services. The actions themselves will need to be bold and creative, and will need to go to the heart of the most critical needs of the most challenged workforce segments.

A recent move by Advocate Aurora Health offers one example of targeted and bold action to fortify the workforce and make a social impact.

Advocate Aurora, which is one of the largest not-for-profit employers in Illinois and Wisconsin, recently announced that it will raise its minimum hourly wage to $18 beginning Dec. 5.[9] The increase will affect 10,800 employees, including those in food service and environmental services positions. An additional 20,000 employees who already make more than $18 an hour, including pharmacy technicians and licensed practical nurses, will also receive raises. The pay increase will cost Advocate Aurora $93 million in the first year.

Why was Advocate Aurora willing to make this investment? In part, it was a workforce issue: the organization wanted to reward valuable work and position itself as a desirable employer. However, it was also a social justice issue. As the organization said in its press release, the investment is intended to "create social impact that dramatically improves individuals' health and well-being." Many of the people holding these positions are members of racial and other groups that have historically been economically disadvantaged. These groups need more money, and Advocate Aurora's investment was a step in that direction.

And why *could* Advocate Aurora make this investment? Not only because of decisive leadership, but also because it is a large organization with an excellent balance sheet. As with so many other organizational challenges and opportunities, scale and astute financial management pave the way to solutions and innovation.

Ultimately, the organizations that succeed in hiring and retention will be the ones that do not view their workforces as a single homogenized group. Successful organizations will dig deep. They will identify key segments. They will hold focus groups on those segments. They will determine what it is that really makes a good job for very different people in their organizations. And then they will respond by delivering tailored changes that are creative, contemporary, and meaningful.

References

1 *Quits Levels and Rates by Industry and Region, Seasonally Adjusted.* Bureau of Labor Statistics, May 1, 2024.

2 Cook, I.: "Who Is Driving the Great Resignation?" *Harvard Business Review,* Sept. 15, 2021.

3 Saad, L., Wigert, B.: "Remote Work Persisting and Trending Permanent." Gallup, Oct. 13, 2021.

4 Verlaine, J. , Benoit, D.: "JPMorgan, Goldman Call Time on Work-From-Home. Their Rivals Are Ready to Pounce." *The Wall Street Journal,* Jul. 6, 2021.

5 Saad, L., Wigert, B.: "Remote Work Persisting and Trending Permanent." Gallup, Oct. 13, 2021.

6 Coate, P.: "Remote Work Before, During, and After the Pandemic." National Council on Compensation Insurance, Jan. 25, 2021.

7 Heggeness, M., Fields, J., Garcia Trejo, Y.A., Schulzetenberg, A.: *Tracking Job Losses for Mothers of School-Age Children During a Health Crisis.* U.S. Census Bureau, Mar. 3, 2021.

8 Gould, E., Wilson, V.: "Black Workers Face Two of the Most Lethal Preexisting Conditions for Coronavirus—Racism and Economic Inequality." Economic Policy Institute, Jun. 1, 2020.

9 "Advocate Aurora Health raises minimum wage to $18/hour." Advocate Health Care, press release, Nov. 11, 2021.

Skeptics Wanted

JANUARY 19, 2021

"Intellectuals are most valued when the dominant paradigm begins to break down."
    —Paul Yingling, quoted in *The Generals* by Thomas E. Ricks[1]

The concepts of "organizational thinking" and "organizational learning" have been around for several decades. Peter Senge coined the phrase "learning organization" in his 1990 book *The Fifth Discipline*,[2] and the more recent influx of business-intelligence solutions has put a big-data spin on the concept.

However, never before have organizations been required to think more rapidly and radically than in the volatile environment of COVID-19, when existing business models are being decimated daily, and organizations need to hit a new target that is hazy at best.

War is an apt metaphor for the situation that organizations—very much including hospitals and health systems—face today. In war, leaders must plan for and react to forces that are volatile and uncertain. That description is fully appropriate for the growing and morphing crisis of COVID-19.

In such situations, organizational thinking is a crucial to both the *process* and *outcomes* of leadership. This point is hammered home repeatedly in the book *The Generals* by Thomas E. Ricks, which is not only a insightful work of military history, but one of the best leadership books you will ever read.

Everybody Starts Wrong

"Usually, everyone gets it wrong at the beginning of a war," Ricks writes, paraphrasing military historian Sir Michael Howard.[3] Faced with a highly complex and unpredictable situation, being right at the outset is, according to Ricks, "an almost impossible task."

Howard observes, "When everybody starts wrong, the advantage goes to the side which can most quickly adjust itself to the new and unfamiliar environment and learn from its mistakes." To make those adjustments, Howard goes on, requires an organizational capacity to "get it right quickly when the moment arrives." And that requires an organizational capability to *think,* and think quickly.

Which begs the question: *how?*

Intellectuals and Skeptics

This kind of in-the-moment thinking cannot be achieved from a standing start. It is a quality that successful organizations nurture over the long term. And that means nurturing two types of individuals that I fear are a disappearing breed in too many organizations: intellectuals and skeptics.

According to Ricks, based on his study, successful commanders "cultivate and maintain cultures in which their subordinates feel free to exercise initiative and speak their minds freely." This cultivation includes, writes Ricks, keeping "alive the careers of outliers and innovators."

This is a tall order for executives who, on any given day, are moving rapidly from meeting to meeting, from tough decision to tough decision. In such an environment, rapid consensus can feel necessary just to make it through the day. The presence of individuals who want to introduce a different context, a contrasting viewpoint, or new data points can certainly slow down progress toward consensus. However, these people are absolutely necessary when a crisis arises.

Paul Yingling was a Lieutenant Colonel in the U.S. Army who had three deployments in Iraq and, toward the end of his career, was highly critical of the conventional wisdom and lack of innovative thinking of military leadership.

Yingling wrote, "Intellectuals are most valued when the dominant paradigm begins to break down. In this moment of crisis, the heretics become the heroes, as they have already constructed alternative paradigms that others haven't considered."[4]

From this observation, Yingling draws one of the most important lessons for leadership: *"In large organizations, the challenge is to keep the skeptics from becoming extinct."*

Leading Through Crisis

After almost a year, daily COVID cases and hospitalizations are spiking. The vaccination rollout so far has been rocky. And even the CEO of Moderna says, "We are going to live with this virus, we think, forever."[5]

The efforts of hospitals and health systems have been nothing short of heroic. However, the escalating nature of this crisis continues to present the greatest leadership challenge hospitals have ever faced. Every facet of the traditional operating model is being challenged—care models, staffing, facilities, technology, communication, and on and on.

More than ever before, hospital leaders need new ideas. As Yingling said, the old paradigms are breaking down. We need people who are skeptical of the conventional wisdom. We need people who have been thinking for years about new healthcare delivery models. We need people who have new perspectives. We need people with new skill sets. If these people don't exist within our organizations, we need to bring them into the fold. We need to nurture these people like never before by giving them a platform for testing new ideas and an open channel to share their questions and insights at the highest levels of the organization.

In a crisis, we cannot afford for "organizational thinking" to be just a platitude. It must be a core organizational capability.

References

1 Ricks, T.E.: *The Generals: American Military Command from World War II to Today*, Penguin Books, 2013.

2 Senge, P.: *The Fifth Discipline: The Art & Practice of The Learning Organization*, Doubleday, 2006.

3 Ricks, T.E.: *The Generals: American Military Command from World War II to Today*, Penguin Books, 2013.

4 Ricks, T.E.: *The Generals: American Military Command from World War II to Today*, Penguin Books, 2013.

5 Lovelace Jr., B.: "Moderna CEO Says the World Will Have to Live with Covid 'Forever.'" CNBC, Jan. 31, 2021.

The Role of Not-for-Profit Healthcare

In Defense of Not-for-Profit Healthcare

OCTOBER 5, 2022

How soon they forget. Throughout 2020 and 2021, the media was full of praise for hospitals and healthcare workers on the frontlines of the COVID-19 pandemic.

When the pandemic was new in the spring of 2020, Americans were effusive in their appreciation of hospitals and the people who worked in them. At that time, a COVID vaccine was a distant dream, and personal protective equipment was so scarce it had to be rationed and reused. To all who valued the safety of home in those early days, it was clear that healthcare workers weren't running away from danger; they were running toward it.

In New York City, which was the U.S. pandemic epicenter that spring, a curious ritual played out every evening at 7 o'clock. People emerged from quarantine onto balconies, fire escapes, front stoops, and rooftops to cheer for their city's healthcare heroes using whatever makeshift noisemakers they could find. They shared videos of these flash events on social media. Later, as the pandemic spread across the country, yard signs popped up in cities large and small: "A healthcare hero lives here"…"Thank you, healthcare heroes." Press coverage conveyed a sense of awe at both the personal sacrifices and the heroic efforts healthcare workers made on a daily basis.

That was then. This is now: We are currently witnessing a media free-for-all challenging the tax-exempt status, financial practices, and ostensible market power of not-for-profit hospitals and health systems. This is happening despite the fact that thousands of Americans are still hospitalized with the COVID-19 virus and more than 400 are dying of it on any given day. And despite the fact that America's hospitals are dealing with an exceptional and unexpected aftermath of the pandemic.

Today, the financial health of America's hospitals is in serious jeopardy. Indeed, our projections show that 2022 is shaping up as the worst financial year for hospitals in memory.[1] In the first six months of 2022, hospital operating margins fell 102% compared with pre-pandemic levels. Median operating margins for hospitals have been negative through all of 2022. Through the end of 2022, hospitals are projected to lose billions of dollars with no foreseeable federal support. Expenses are projected to increase nearly $135 billion over 2021 levels. More than half of hospitals are projected to have negative operating margins in 2022.

At the same time, shortages of nurses and other clinicians are putting severe pressure on clinical teams and creating backlogs of patients in desperate need of hospital beds. As one hospital nurse put it, "We're drowning."[2]

There are other, more nuanced stories behind healthcare industry headlines. For example, media commentators often applaud the big-tech companies disrupting healthcare, such as Amazon,[3] Google, and Apple, for their customer-centric, technology-savvy approach to healthcare. What doesn't get mentioned is what hospitals do every day that these other companies do not and will not: Take care of people with the most critical ill patients requiring the most sophisticated treatments and procedures. Take care of people who do not have insurance or the means to pay. And do all that 24 hours a day in a face-to-face environment. These big tech players don't have the costly stand-ready responsibilities or the duty to provide unprofitable but medically essential services that hospitals do.

We as a society need to realize that all of these "must have" clinical services, which we and our families depend on in every kind of healthcare situation, don't just magically appear. It requires the work and cooperation and self-sacrifice of doctors, frontline healthcare workers, administrators and Board members. It requires enough money, the right facilities, and some of the most complex processes and procedures operating within any part of our overall economy. It requires the hardest of hard work each and every day.

During a period marked by both existential challenges and daily crises, our country's hospitals and healthcare workers found a multitude of ways to meet the moment, and without question saved countless lives. But hospitals and healthcare workers aren't looking for impromptu serenades. Or even yard signs. They're just doing their jobs. Hospitals and healthcare workers are simply looking for our support and validation in the face of extreme economic and organizational headwinds.

The cooperation, the support, and the best thoughts and intentions of all who are involved in the American healthcare system, from those who provide the care to those who provide the funding and to the patients who participate, are essential for that system to be one we can all be proud of.

References

[1] *The Current State of Hospital Finances: Fall 2022 Update*, Kaufman Hall & Associates, 2022.

[2] Templeton, A.: "With Too Many Patients and Too Few Colleagues, Oregon Nurses Say: 'We're Drowning.'" Oregon Public Broadcasting, Sept. 6, 2022.

[3] Kaufman, K., Bates, M., Clarin, D., Fromberg, R.: "Amazon and One Medical: What's Going on Here?" Kaufman Hall, Jul. 27, 2022.

A Leadership Playbook for Equity

APRIL 27, 2022

When it comes to equity, healthcare organizations face three different and very difficult challenges: health disparities among patient populations, income inequality in the healthcare workforce, and of diversity in the C-suite and the boardroom.

To get the job done, you have to tackle all three. And that takes an uncommon—even selfless—type of leadership.

In his recent decision to retire from coaching, Tampa Bay Buccaneers head coach Bruce Arians showed what that kind of leadership looks like. If you follow football, you know that Arians' retirement announcement came as a surprise, if not a shock, to the NFL community. With a stellar 80-48-1 career win-loss record, a Super Bowl victory in 2021, and the recent return of superstar quarterback Tom Brady, Arians had good prospects of coaching the Bucs to another Super Bowl victory next year. That would have virtually assured his ascension to the Pro Football Hall of Fame.

But Arians had a different kind of legacy in mind.

After assembling one of the most diverse staffs in football, Arians saw an opportunity to elevate defensive coordinator Todd Bowles, his handpicked successor, at a time when the Bucs were poised for success. Surely it was clear to Arians that no one is tackling the abysmal diversity hiring record in the NFL in a meaningful way despite the recent lawsuit alleging discriminatory hiring practices by the league.[1] Of 500-plus head coaches in the NFL since its inception in 1920, just 24 were Black and most of those held interim positions.[2] Bowles is one of only four Blacks who are currently working as a head coach.

Arians saw an opportunity to be part of the solution and he seized it. He timed it when the team was well situated, knowing that Black head coaches rarely get the second chances with other teams that whites do when their teams don't succeed.

Solving equity—whether in football or in healthcare—requires having the right values, making the right decisions, and implementing those decisions. By his actions, Arians came through on all counts. He went a step further by recognizing that it's not enough to give people from underrepresented groups a chance; they need and deserve a chance to *succeed*.

The NFL was supposed to have a structural solution for diversity in the head coaching ranks. The Rooney Rule, established in 2003, required that any NFL team with a head coach opening must include at least one diverse candidate among its slate of interviewees. I think everyone would agree that the Rooney Rule has been a failure—that including a diverse candidate did not create a situation in which a minority candidate was actually hired and, when hired, was successful.

In the absence of a structural solution for diversity among NFL head coaches, Arians substituted his own personal level of leadership. The NFL is not alone in this regard. No industry vertical has come up with that solution, including healthcare. While we continue to look for those structural solutions, the kind of strategic leadership shown by Arians appears to be the way forward.

Healthcare leaders can take a page from Arians' playbook to address all three types of equity challenges in healthcare.

Health disparities. People in healthcare circles have been talking about the zip code effect for years.[3] Zip code is a proxy for a series of health inequities that have plagued marginalized communities of color for decades, affecting a person's health and life expectancy more than any other factor. Soon after the COVID-19 pandemic began, it became clear that Blacks and Latinos were being hospitalized and dying at much higher rates than whites. At that point, it became impossible to rationalize health disparities any longer.

Income inequality. About 4.5 million people working in healthcare settings are considered low-wage workers, defined as the bottom 20% of wage earners.[4] Deemed essential workers during the pandemic, they include nursing assistants and aides as well as environmental services, laundry and food service workers. These frontline workers, who are disproportionately female, Black and Latino, are not compensated at a level that they can effectively manage within our economy. The pathway to income equity for these workers remains unclear.

Diversity in leadership. At the C-suite level, progress in improving diversity has been slow. An analysis of leadership diversity in 100 leading hospitals found that only 6% of CEOs were Black.[5] Just 18% of hospitals had at least one Black leader in a common C-suite role. The highest percentage of Black leaders in a C-suite role was in diversity/equity. Women are also under-represented at the executive level. Although they hold three-quarters of healthcare jobs,[6] only 15% of healthcare organization CEOs are female.[7]

If you want to move the needle on diversity, having the right values is the starting point. But unless you make decisions based on those values and implement those decisions strategically, as Bruce Arians did, we will be having the same conversations about healthcare equity in five years that we're having now.

References

1   Belson, K., Vrentas, J.: "Brian Flores Sues N.F.L., Claiming Bias in Coaching Search." *The New York Times*, Feb. 1, 2022.

2   Kimbrough, J.: "Every Black Head Coach in the History of The NFL!" ROAR Detroit, Feb. 4, 2022.

3   Kaufman, K.: "COVID-19 and Black Lives Matter Lay Bare the Need for Healthcare Change." Kaufman Hall, Jul. 13, 2020.

4   Garfield, R., Rae, M., Claxton, G., Orgera, K.: "Double Jeopardy: Low Wage Workers at Risk for Health and Financial Implications of COVID-19." Kaiser Family Foundation, Apr. 29, 2020.

5   *Black Representation in the C-Suite*, The Chartis Group, May 25, 2021.

6   *Getting Real About Inclusive Leadership*, Catalyst, Nov. 21, 2019.

7   Odei, B.C., Seldon, C., Fernandez, M.: "Representation of Women in the Leadership Structure of the US Health Care System," *JAMA Open Network* 4(11), Nov. 9, 2021.

The New Public Health Imperative for Hospitals

FEBRUARY 16, 2022

One of the COVID pandemic's most bitter lessons has been the complete inadequacy and dysfunction of the U.S. public health system, if the word "system" can even be applied. Prior to COVID, these shortcomings were hiding in plain sight. Now, they are evident to all and exacerbated as the nation struggles to protect the health of its citizens in the face of a pandemic entering its third year.

At the outset of the pandemic, research showed a $4.5 billion funding shortfall to provide what authors of a study in *The Milbank Quarterly* called "a minimum standard of foundational public health capabilities."[1] Further, more than 85% of public health funding comes from state and local sources, leading to significant variation by geography. For example, states including New York, New Hampshire, and Montana spend more than $129 per person to public health, while states including Nevada, Missouri, and Indiana spend less than $59.

This geographic variation in funding indicates a significant inequity in the types and levels of public health services. Certainly, the existing public health infrastructure did not protect historically vulnerable populations from the effects of COVID, with Hispanic and Black individuals at least twice as likely to die from COVID as whites and almost three times as likely to be hospitalized, according to a Kaiser Family Foundation analysis of CDC data.[2]

Public health agencies also suffer from chronic understaffing. In the decade prior to COVID, state public health agencies lost 16% of their full-time positions,[3] and county and city public health agencies lost 20% of their positions in the past 15 years.[4]

The result has been an inadequate, unequitable, and fragmented collection of services that, when COVID hit, was unable to deliver what the country desperately needed: prompt, consistent, and widespread testing and vaccination; effective contact tracing; and clear communication with the public about healthy practices.

The politicization of health has made a bad situation worse. As of September 2021, 26 states passed laws that limited public health powers,[5] and 303 state and local public health department leaders resigned, retired, or had been fired.

Hospitals have always been the organizations that truly matter when it comes to healthcare delivery. And now, highlighted by COVID, hospitals have become the organizations that truly matter when it comes to public health.

Consider some of the core services of public health, as defined by the CDC:[6]

- Assess and monitor population health status, factors that influence health, and community needs and assets
- Investigate, diagnose, and address health problems and hazards affecting the population
- Communicate effectively to inform and educate people about health, factors that influence it, and how to improve it
- Strengthen, support, and mobilize communities and partnerships to improve health
- Assure an effective system that enables equitable access to the individual services and care needed to be healthy

- Improve and innovate public health functions through ongoing evaluation, research, and continuous quality improvement
- Build and maintain a strong organizational infrastructure for public health

Over time, many of these services have become a more common part of health systems' purview. The slow but inexorable shift of financial risk from insurers to providers has created the economic incentive for hospitals and health systems to better understand population health status and the specific factors that influence it; to enhance access to care particularly in underserved areas; and to reach out into communities to manage health risks before they produce the need for more intensive levels of intervention.

Perhaps more important than economic incentive has been the mission incentive of not-for-profit providers. Almost universally, not-for-profit hospitals and health systems articulate a mission to improve the health and wellbeing of communities. Increasingly, this mission has led hospitals into the challenging public health arena.

The COVID crisis has taken these new health system responsibilities to a different level. Health systems were instrumental in developing and administering COVID tests, tracing COVID's path, educating communities about the virus and how to avoid it, and providing front-line care for the huge swath of Americans affected by the virus.

Moving forward, hospitals will be asked by communities all over the country to be the organizations that deal with a broader set of national problems related to the wellbeing of patients and communities—problems that COVID has made much worse, problems that the public sector has never been able to solve.

With this new set of responsibilities comes an entirely new set of strategic, operational, and financial implications for hospitals and health systems. Meeting these challenges will require a new level of health system ideas, a new level of health system aggressiveness, and a new level of health system ambition. More than ever, health systems will need to have to address social determinants of health; access and analyze data about health conditions, reimagine access to preventive care, develop care models tailored to specific populations. The costs will be enormous, and the need for intellectual capital considerable.

America is looking to someone or something to take on what is now a paramount set of national healthcare problems. It is up to the hospital sector to bring its charitable mission, its resources, and its passion to bear on this awesome responsibility.

References

1   Maani, N., Galea, S.: "COVID-19 and Underinvestment in the Public Health Infrastructure of the United States." *The Milbank Quarterly*, Jun. 2020.

2   Hill, L., Artiga, S.: "COVID-19 Cases and Deaths by Race/Ethnicity: Current Data and Changes Over Time." *Kaiser Family Foundation*, Aug, 22, 2022.

3   Ollove, M., Vestal, C.: "Public Health Systems Still Aren't Ready for the Next Pandemic." Stateline, Jan. 27, 2021.

4   Bryant, B.: "Protect Funding for Core Local Public Health Services and Prevention Programs." National Association of Counties, Jan. 23, 2024.

5   Weber, L., Barry-Jester, A.M.: "Most States Have Cut Back Public Health Powers Amid Pandemic." Associated Press, Sept. 15, 2021.

6   "10 Essential Public Health Services." Centers for Disease Control and Prevention, May 15, 2024.

Taking a No-Regrets Approach to Health Inequity

DECEMBER 15, 2021

I recently finished Denis Johnson's National Book Award-winning novel about the Vietnam War, *Tree of Smoke*.[1] Toward the end of the book, the narrator quotes an aphorism that I found particularly apt for today: "Don't interrogate your opportunities; it's not what you do that you regret, it's what you don't do."

In the book, this insight is meant as a personal philosophy, a way of thinking about one's life and accomplishments, about decisions made and decisions not made. However, it could just as easily apply to organizations, particularly in healthcare.

For many years, healthcare organizations have faced a set of historically intractable problems, some of which have become far more apparent and intense in the 20 months since the onset of the COVID-19 pandemic, including dealing with the fallout of a public health system that is fragmented, understaffed, and wholly inadequate to the challenges brought forward by the pandemic.[2]

A central problem, one that runs through public health, workforce, and many other issues, is the health and healthcare inequities arising from pernicious disparities based on individual's race or ethnicity, as well as gender, sexual identity, age, disability, socioeconomic status, and geographic location.[3]

The evidence of health and healthcare inequity is staggering. (The statistics cited in this article come from a new book called *Unequal Cities*, which I highly recommend.)[4]

The mortality rate for Blacks is about one-quarter higher than for whites. In the United States as a whole, annual excess deaths of Black Americans due to higher Black mortality rates is a shocking *192 preventable deaths per day* or *8 preventable deaths per hour.* The number of years of life lost due to preventable death for Black Americans is 59% higher than for whites.

The mortality rate from heart disease is 30% higher for Blacks than for whites, and the mortality rate for cancer is 20% higher. Annually in the U.S. there are *32,883 more preventable deaths* among Blacks than whites from heart disease and cancer.

These disparities vary significantly depending on where you live. The average difference in life expectancy for Blacks and whites among the 29 largest cities in the country is 4 years. However, in Washington, D.C., the difference is 12 years—a 73-year life expectancy for Blacks compared with 85 years for Whites. In San Francisco the difference is 10.5 years, in Los Angeles 9.5 years, and in Chicago 8.3 years. Mortality rates from heart disease for Blacks in Washington, DC, is 144% higher than for whites, compared with an 8% difference in Baltimore.

In this context, the notion of interrogating your options and regretting what you don't do is not just philosophical. It has actual results on people's lives.

How much responsibility should healthcare organizations assume for solving the problem of health inequity? One view is that responsibility should be shared among the public sector, the private sector, and healthcare organizations. That is an understandable view, and is indeed the status quo. Health inequity is enormously complex and pervasive; it touches on agencies, companies, and individuals throughout the country. However, shared responsibility has not solved the problem, in part because there has not been a single point of accountability. No one has stepped up and said, We will be accountable.

Healthcare organizations need to simplify their thinking about health inequity. They need to say, One of our most crucial responsibilities going forward over the next decade is to solve this problem. We will not over-interrogate this opportunity, as healthcare organizations are prone to do. We are going to take all the necessary actions that we have the power and authority to take. And although we are more than willing to work cooperatively with all of the different constituencies we need to work with, we're not going to wait. We're going to jump in and figure out how to solve this. When it comes to solving the problem of health inequity, we are not going to regret the things that we did not do.

References

1 Johnson, D.: *Tree of Smoke: A Novel*. Picador, 2008.

2 Ollove, M., Vestal, C.: "Public Health Systems Still Aren't Ready for the Next Pandemic." Stateline, Jan. 27, 2021.

3 *Disparities*. HealthyPeople.gov, 2020.

4 Benjamins, M.R., De Maio, F.G. (eds.): *Unequal Cities: Structural Racism and the Death Gap in America's Largest Cities*. Hopkins Press, 2021.

COVID and Black Lives Matter Lay Bare the Need for Healthcare Change

JULY 13, 2020

We have known for years that a person's zip code has more to do with health and life expectancy than any other factor.

A look at just one city illustrates this situation in profound and disturbing terms.[1] In the affluent Chicago Loop, the diabetes rate is 2%. In poverty-stricken South Chicago, it's 26%. In the Edison Park neighborhood, the asthma hospitalization rate is 3%. In West Englewood, it's 73%. And most disturbing of all, in the desirable neighborhood of Streeterville, life expectancy is 90 years, while 10 miles away in struggling Englewood, life expectancy is 60 years.

Not surprisingly, the populations in neighborhoods with better health and longer life expectancy tend to be predominantly White, while the populations in neighborhoods with worse health and shorter life expectancy tend to be predominantly people of color.

Nationwide, the demographic data have long told a story of racial disparities in quality of care and in rates of morbidity and mortality from cancers, heart disease, and maternal and child health. These health disparities take a toll every day throughout the country.

When these disparities are combined with a major health epidemic like COVID-19, the results are especially discriminating and jarring. Three times more Blacks and Latinos than Whites have been diagnosed with COVID-19—this applies in communities of all types, and all across the country.[2] And Blacks have died from COVID at more than four times the rate as Whites among ages 75 to 84 and more than two times the rate as Whites ages 85 and older.[3]

Now the Black Lives Matter movement has put an even brighter light on society's structural racism—a condition that has long contributed to racial disparities in health and healthcare. In 2002, the Institute of Medicine released a report titled *Unequal Treatment* that found, "bias, prejudice, and stereotyping on the part of healthcare providers may contribute to differences in care."[4]

On one level, changing this deeply embedded dynamic requires a new structure and approach to managing healthcare in America's most disadvantaged communities. What is actually required: a robust ambulatory care network, a care management system that targets specific conditions and populations with a coordinated approach to health promotion and health care, and resources to address environmental factors and other social determinants of health such as food, adequate housing, and air quality.

However, ending racial disparities in healthcare is not just a function of resources and strategy. Equally important is a change in awareness, beliefs, and behaviors. Just as society as a whole is coming to grips with structural racism, the nation's entire healthcare system must confront its own biases and how those biases affect all aspects of care from access to diagnosis to treatment.

Whatever effort has been made to date to assure racial equity within our healthcare system has clearly not been sufficient. To make good on the promise to deliver the same access and quality of care to all citizens, America's healthcare system must make racial equity part of its day-to-day DNA. And to accomplish that new systemic DNA, the entire system of care requires more people of color in leadership positions. This includes at the board of directors level, in the C-suite, at the bedside, inside critical governmental agencies, and throughout associations and professional service organizations.

I strongly suspect that many healthcare organizations of all stripes and types are currently moving to address issues of racial equity by giving the entire problem greater visibility and impact within their organizations' strategic plans. But we all know that the intent and emphasis of strategic plans tend to ebb and flow over time. What is critical in one year may be much less important in the next. What is absolutely necessary is to stop seeing racial equity as just another page in a long and complex strategic plan, and instead see that racial-equity page as the permanent cover of every healthcare organization's strategic book.

References

1 *City Health Dashboard*, NYU Grossman School of Medicine, Department of Population Health.

2 Oppel Jr., J.A., Gebeloff, R., Lai, K.K.R., Wright, W., Smith, M.: "The Fullest Look Yet at the Racial Inequity of Coronavirus." *The New York Times*, Jul. 5, 2020.

3 Ford, R., Reber, S., Reeves, R.V.: "Race Gaps in COVID-19 Deaths Are Even Bigger Than They Appear." *The Brookings Institution*, Jun. 16, 2020.

4 *Unequal Treatment: What Healthcare Providers Need to Know About Racial and Ethnic Disparities in Healthcare*. National Institutes of Medicine, Mar. 2020.

A Path Forward for Rural Healthcare

APRIL 24, 2019

With Kenneth Beutke, president, OSF HealthCare Saint Elizabeth Medical Center, Ottawa, Ill.; James Landman, Senior Vice President, Kaufman Hall; and Erik Thorsen, chief executive officer, Columbia Memorial Hospital, Astoria, Ore.

Rural America encompasses a broad geography. Almost 20 percent of the U.S. population lives within the 84 percent of the nation's land area that the Federal Office of Rural Health Policy (FORHP) defines as rural.[1] But rural America is a very diverse place, and there is no single solution that will address the healthcare needs of the people who live there.

Two of this article's coauthors—Ken Beutke and Erik Thorsen—are rural health executives. Ken is president of 97-bed OSF HealthCare OSF Saint Elizabeth Medical Center in Ottawa, Ill., and also oversees a facility that was recently converted from a hospital to a rural health center in Streator, Ill. Both Ottawa and Streator are in LaSalle County (Ottawa, the larger of the two, is the county seat). Erik is CEO of 25-bed Columbia Memorial Hospital in Astoria, Ore., the county seat of Clatsop County.

There are several similarities between the two counties that Ken's and Erik's facilities serve. Both are designated "micropolitan areas" by the U.S. Census Bureau—in other words, both counties have an urban core of at least 10,000 but not more than 50,000 people. Both have populations that trend slightly older than the U.S. average of 15.6 percent of the population above age 65 (the figures are 18.5 percent for LaSalle County and 21.7 percent for Clatsop County). Both are approximately 100 miles away from major metropolitan areas (Chicago and Portland). In both counties, per capita and median household incomes are slightly below the national average, while broadband internet access is very close to the national average of 78.1 percent of households.[2]

But there are also important differences between the counties. Although designated as rural, LaSalle County in fact has a higher population density than the U.S. national average, with just over 100 people per square mile (the U.S. average is 87.5 people per square mile). Clatsop County's population density is significantly below the national average, with 44.7 people per square mile. LaSalle County's population is slowly declining, with a negative 3.4 percent change in population from 2010 to 2017. Clatsop County's population is growing; in the same period, its population grew by 5.8 percent, slightly ahead of the U.S. national population growth rate of 5.5 percent.

The trends we see in LaSalle and Clatsop counties are representative of differences in rural areas nationwide. The U.S. Department of Agriculture confirms that while the vast majority of older-age counties are rural, one-third of these counties are retirement destinations or have developed recreation-based economies. These counties have seen an upturn in population growth since 2012, similar to what we are seeing in Clatsop County, Ore. In contrast, another third of older-age counties are "persistent population loss" areas, which have been subject to long-term out-migration by young adults. LaSalle County, Ill., may not yet be witnessing persistent population loss, but it is experiencing gradual population decline.[3]

The different population dynamics across rural areas is one of many factors that call for different approaches to address the healthcare needs of rural residents. Some approaches will require change at the national policy level, particularly those touching upon the Medicare program, which is the primary payer for many rural hospitals. Other approaches should be taken up at the state level or by individual organizations, which are better situated to tailor efforts to the needs, opportunities, and challenges of different rural communities.

Challenges to the Future of Rural Healthcare

Provider organizations in rural America are subject to the same forces that are reshaping healthcare across the nation. Demand for inpatient services is weakening as many procedures and services migrate to outpatient settings and other alternative sites of care. The aging of the Baby Boom generation is shifting payer mix away from commercial insurance to Medicare. Technological advancement is enabling new models of healthcare delivery that have the potential to significantly disrupt traditional delivery models.

Although these trends are affecting provider organizations in communities of all sizes, they can have a unique or magnified impact on rural healthcare providers:

- *Declining demand for inpatient care.* Many critical access hospitals already have very low daily censuses. The national average daily census for all CAHs nationwide in 2016 was 2.7 acute beds.[4] Further volume declines threaten not only the financial viability of low-census CAHs, but also the quality of care available to patients.

- *Shifting payer mix.* With populations that tend to be older than the national average,[5] many rural areas will feel the impact of the shift of patients from commercial insurance to Medicare more acutely than metropolitan or suburban areas. Even in growing rural areas, that impact will be felt more strongly to the extent that growth is being driven by retirees.

- *Technological advancements.* The needs of rural patients were an early driving force in the development of telemedicine. Further advances in virtual care delivery may well have a disproportionate impact on more geographically isolated rural areas, especially if broadband access and related connectivity issues can be resolved.[6]

Given these pressures, significant change in the nature and delivery of rural healthcare is inevitable. While attempts to preserve the status quo are understandable, they can also put off necessary discussion of what the future of rural health might be.

The Future of the Rural Hospital

Reports on rural health often start with statistics on the number of hospitals that have closed, or are threatened by closure, in rural communities. It is true that, as of February 2019, there have been 97 rural hospital closures since January 2010. It is also true that, of these 97, only 57 facilities completely shut down. Five were converted to nursing or rehabilitation facilities; 16 were converted to outpatient/primary care/rural health center use; and 19 were converted to urgent or emergency care facilities.[7] The most relevant question is not how many hospitals closed. Rather, it is whether the residents of affected communities retained access to facilities and services that meet their healthcare needs.

The hospital in Streator, Ill., was one of the 97 to close since 2010; it is also one of the 16 closed hospitals that have been converted to outpatient, primary care, or rural health center use. The decision to close a hospital is never easy. Hospitals are often among the largest employers in a rural community, and local businesses often feel a full-service hospital is needed to draw companies for economic development. Based on several factors, however, we believe the decision to convert the hospital to a rural health center with 24/7 emergency care will be the right decision for Streator in the long term.

First, Streator residents will continue to have access to emergency care and other essential services through the new health center. Continued access to emergency care was the greatest concern of Streator residents, and was among the first commitments OSF HealthCare made to the community.

Second, the decision had minimal impact on employment. When OSF HealthCare acquired the Streator hospital, employment was down to 200 employees. OSF has been able to retain approximately 180 of these employees to staff the services it has in place or is planning for the new rural health center.

Third, Streator is in an area that is over-bedded. Within a 25-mile radius of Streator are the 97-bed OSF Saint Elizabeth hospital in Ottawa, Ill., and the 42-bed OSF Saint James hospital in Pontiac, Ill; two other hospitals are 35 miles to the northwest. The health system that ran the hospital simply could not maintain sufficient volumes to make the facility financially viable. By taking control of the site, OSF HealthCare had an opportunity to rationalize services within a local network of hospitals and other providers. Travel times to the hospitals in Ottawa and Pontiac are comparable to travel times many individuals in the Chicago metropolitan area encounter, and 24/7 emergency services remain available to Streator residents if travel to a hospital is not feasible.

In short, conversion of the Streator hospital to a health center with a free-standing rural emergency facility helped the community avoid the two greatest impacts associated with rural hospital closures: lost access to emergency care and the economic impact of lost jobs. And, as described later in this article, it has converted excess inpatient space into space that better supports the community's long-term health.

Conversion of the Streator facility could serve as a model for other health systems seeking to rationalize the provision of services within an owned network of rural facilities. A health system can provide clinical, financial, operational, and technological support to a rural health center, with the center in turn serving as spoke to the hub of larger facilities within the system's network. Within the context of a system as a whole, a rural health center's return on investment can be tied to downstream revenues resulting from referrals, or to savings realized under a system's managed or accountable care contracts resulting from a health center's focus on improving community health.

Without the backing of a health system, or the opportunity to capture downstream revenues or savings, independent rural hospitals have more limited options, particularly in communities that face both declining populations and declining inpatient volumes. One possible solution—found in both the Medicare Payment Advisory Commission's recommendations to Congress[8] and the bipartisan-sponsored but not yet passed Rural Emergency Acute Care Hospital (REACH) Act[9]—would end the requirement that rural hospitals maintain inpatient beds to receive Medicare payments. Instead, rural hospitals could convert to stand-alone emergency departments, with the option of changing back to an inpatient hospital if circumstances change. A converted facility would still be able to offer ambulance and outpatient services and be paid for these services as well as for emergency care.

The future of the rural hospital will be brightest in areas that are experiencing population growth. In areas were population growth is flat or declining, the number of hospitals that can be sustained by the local population likely will continue to shrink. Whether those hospitals close for good or are converted to facilities that can still address essential community healthcare needs will depend on the ability of larger health systems to grow and support the conversion of facilities in their networks, or the willingness of legislators to support a more flexible model for rural healthcare facilities.

The Sustainability of Market-based Competition

We believe that competitive markets are a good thing. But healthcare is susceptible to a range of market failures that can be especially acute in rural areas. For example, a healthy market can adjust supply to meet demand. But physicians in a number of specialties—particularly primary care—are already in short supply. In rural areas that face heightened recruitment and retention challenges, the problem of supply is even more acute. Of the approximately 7,000 designated Health Professional Shortage Areas (HPSAs) in the U.S., more than 4,600—just over 65 percent—are in rural or partially rural areas.[10]

Healthy markets also require competition. But it is unrealistic to expect competition to work in rural markets that may struggle to sustain one hospital, let alone two. Where there is competition among hospitals in rural areas, the effect may be more to limit the services that the competitors can offer than to expand access to care.

It all comes down to numbers. Certain services require a minimum number of physicians simply to handle call coverage. At Columbia Memorial Hospital, for example, the obstetrics practice and general surgery practice require at least four to five physicians on staff to ensure call coverage. The other critical number is volume. If volumes are not sufficient, patients justifiably might start to question the quality of care. Columbia Memorial has good volume: its obstetricians deliver approximately 300 babies each year, and its orthopedics practice has two physicians who each perform between three and six procedures a week. If these numbers were to decline significantly, however, the hospital would have to question the viability of continuing these services.

Columbia Memorial has competition with two other critical access hospitals within an approximately 30-mile radius; it is fortunate to be the largest provider in a rural area that is growing and has been able to sustain a competitive model. But in other rural communities that face greater difficulties recruiting and retaining physicians or declining volumes, duplicative services within an area that could be served by a single facility multiplies the number of physicians the facilities need to recruit. Moreover, competition for already thin volumes increases the likelihood that no facility will be able to have adequate volumes to ensure consistent quality of care or sustain a financially viable practice. As noted in a recent *New York Times* article, the pressures of clinician shortages, dwindling volumes, and declining revenues are already creating "care deserts" for obstetric services in rural areas.[11]

Favoring collaboration over competition might better meet the needs of rural communities. Rural residents need access to essential services such as emergency care, diagnostic services, primary care, behavioral health, rehabilitation services, and certain specialties such as general surgery and obstetrics. Rural communities would also benefit from services that help prevent the need for more acute care. In Streator, OSF HealthCare is promoting a "healthy village" concept that provides space for social service agencies and other collaborating service providers to have a co-located physical home along with OSF-provided services. OSF is also looking at the issue of service duplication across the health system, social service agencies, and other community service providers, and has already worked with the YMCA to adopt programs that OSF had available to streamline provision of those services within the community.

A move from competitive to collaborative frameworks may involve significant trade-offs, including changes to payment structures and heightened state oversight. Changes to payment structures likely would move in the direction of global payments to designated facilities—perhaps existing rural hospitals—that could coordinate care and payments among collaborating providers, social service agencies, and others. In the absence of competition, state oversight likely would include rate setting, but also oversight of clinical outcomes, patient experience, and distribution of healthcare services.

Several states are already moving in this direction. Maryland, which has had an all-payer rate setting system in place for more than 40 years, is now participating with CMS in an all-payer model test that is shifting virtually all hospital revenue into global payment models that incentivize collaboration among providers. Pennsylvania has begun a Rural Health Model with CMS that also uses all-payer global budgets to help stabilize the financial health of rural hospitals and promote collaboration among rural healthcare providers through development of Rural Hospital Transformation Plans. Vermont—a largely rural state—established a board in 2011 with regulatory authority over provider rate-setting and workforce plan approvals, and has now entered an all-payer ACO model with CMS intended "to make redesigning the entire care delivery system a rational business strategy for Vermont providers and payers."

Collaboration and competition need not be mutually exclusive. Columbia Memorial sees opportunities for an improved competitive position through collaboration, and recently strengthened a partnership with Oregon Health & Science University, the state's only academic medical center, which allows more access to specialist care in the local community. And market-based healthcare policy still may be appropriate for larger population centers that can support a sufficient degree of hospital competition across services and attract an adequate supply of healthcare providers. This may include rural markets that are close to major population centers or are experiencing growth that can sustain a competitive model.

In rural areas where both competition and providers are in short supply, however, something along the lines of a public utility approach may be more appropriate to ensure that limited resources are best mobilized to serve the needs of rural residents, and that facilities and providers are able to move forward on a sustainable financial footing.[12] Such an approach could also help ensure adequate distribution of services across rural areas, avoiding "care desert" scenarios that are already developing in service areas such as obstetrics.

The Impact of Disruptive Innovation

The geographic isolation of some rural areas may create a sense of distance from innovations in the healthcare industry, but this is an illusion. It is useful to remember that one of the most significant recent innovations in healthcare—telehealth—had its roots in the need to get medical resources and expertise out into rural areas. The University of Mississippi Medical Center (UMMC) Center for Telehealth—which today is one of only two Telehealth Centers of Excellence recognized by the federal Health Resources & Services Administration—got its start in 2003 with an effort that initially relied on television sets linked to T1 lines to bring emergency care support to rural facilities.[13]

Rural hospitals that have embraced telehealth have discovered several advantages. It can provide patients with access to specialty care that would otherwise be unavailable, and reduce the number of hospital transfers required, allowing rural hospitals to treat more patients in a local setting.[14] Medicare is now paying for certain telehealth services, and will soon pay for more with changes authorized by the 2018 Balanced Budget Act.

Telehealth as it exists today, however, is just the tip of the digital iceberg. As the digital delivery of healthcare advances, rural hospitals may not see the same advantages. Digital management of chronic diseases, direct consumer access to telehealth providers, and other developments in digital healthcare might reduce the need for rural hospital services, regardless of geography. Similarly, the movement of care to retail settings and other emerging on-demand healthcare delivery services[15] may pull more care from rural hospitals, especially in more densely populated rural areas that provide a solid consumer base for these services.

It is impossible to predict exactly how innovation and technological change will affect rural healthcare, but it is clear that change will occur. The question for today is how a rural healthcare facility can establish its value as a hub that facilitates community access to innovation. Columbia Memorial Hospital, for example, has partnered with American Well, a national telehealth provider, to give its patients 24/7 access to its white-label CMH Virtual Care service. The new Streator health center will have dedicated space where patients who do not have at-home internet service can access digital health services. It is also installing a "tech bar" that will help residents learn how to access telehealth services from their home and use wearables for monitoring chronic conditions. Some of these services may reduce demand for care from facilities and local providers, but staying on top of innovation keeps a rural provider relevant in the eyes of the community it serves. And it is better to be a part of change than to be left behind when change occurs.

Significant movement on any of the issues discussed in this article could change the direction taken on others. For example, allowing more flexible facility models that do not require maintenance of inpatient beds could open rural areas to greater competition, as could innovations in digital health that enable national healthcare platforms to compete for business without the constraints of geography.

Today, however, we are very much in a world where on-the-ground delivery of healthcare services matters, and where some rural residents risk losing access to essential healthcare services. Rural healthcare needs new paths forward. These paths will vary, but will require solutions that bring financial stability to rural healthcare providers, support collaborative efforts to address the healthcare needs of rural communities, and give rural healthcare providers the flexibility they need to adapt to changes that are already occurring, and will only accelerate.

1 *Defining Rural Population*. U.S. Health Resources and Services Administration, Jan. 2024.

2 *QuickFacts LaSalle County, Illinois; Clatsop County, Oregon; United States*. U.S. Census Bureau, accessed Feb. 21, 2019.

3 *Rural America at a Glance: 2018 Edition*. United States Department of Agriculture, Economic Research Service: Economic Information Bulletin 200, Nov. 2018. (Older-age counties are those with 20 percent or more of the population aged 65 or older.)

4 *CAH Financial Indicators Report: Summary of Indicator Medians by State*. Flex Monitoring Team , Flex Monitoring Team Data Summary Report No. 26, March 2018.

5 "New Census Data Show Differences Between Urban and Rural Residents." U.S. Census Bureau, press release, Dec. 8, 2016.

6 As of 2016, approximately 14 million rural Americans lacked mobile LTE broadbands at speeds of 10 Mbps/3 Mbps. *2018 Broadband Deployment Report*. Federal Communications Commission, Feb. 2, 2018.

7 "192 Rural Hospital Closures and Conversions since January 2005." University of North Carolina Cecil G. Sheps Center for Health Services Research, accessed Feb. 28, 2019..

8 *Report to the Congress: Medicare and the Health Care Delivery System*. Medicare Payment Advisory Commission, June 2018.

9 S. 1130 (115th): Rural Emergency Acute Care Hospital Act, May 16, 2017.

10 *Designated Health Professional Shortage Areas Statistics*. Bureau of Health Workforce, Health Resources and Services Administration, Mar. 4, 2019.

11 Healy, J.: "It's 4 A.M. The Baby's Coming. But the Hospital Is 100 Miles Away." *The New York Times*, Jul. 17, 2018.

12 For the history and potential future of a public utility model in healthcare, see Bagley, N.: "Medicine as a Public Calling," *Michigan Law Review*, 114(1), 2015.

13 Govindarajan, V., Ramamurti, R.: *Reverse Innovation in Health Care: How to Make Value-Based Delivery Work*. Harvard Business Review Press, 2018.

14 Potter, A., Ward, M., Natafgi, N., Ullrich, F., MacKinney, A., Bell, A, Mueller, K.: "Perceptions of the Benefits of Telemedicine in Rural Communities." *Perspectives in Health Information Management*, Summer 2016.

15 Morrissey, J.: "When the Waiting Room Is Your Living Room." *The New York Times*, Feb. 24, 2019.

FTC Policies Are Big Trouble for Hospitals

FEBRUARY 29, 2016

Healthcare's future is being shaped by some of the biggest companies in the world. However, the Federal Trade Commission seems intent on keeping hospitals from shaping that future.

In April of 2015, IBM launched Watson Health. Less than a year later, IBM has invested more than $4 billion in the division. It acquired Explorys, a cloud-based healthcare intelligence company; Phytel, a population health company; and Merge Healthcare, a provider of enterprise imaging, interoperability and clinical systems. Most recently, it announced plans to acquire Truven Health Analytics for $2.6 billion. Watson Health also has relationships with Apple, Medtronic, Johnson & Johnson, and CVS Health. The division has more than 5,000 employees. "Our goal was to enter the healthcare industry in a big way," said John Kelly, IBM's Senior Vice President of Cognitive Solutions and Research.[1]

Within a three-week period in 2015, three major health insurance mergers were announced: Anthem acquiring Cigna for $54.2 billion,[2] Aetna acquiring Humana for $37 billion,[3] and Centene acquiring Health Net for $6.3 billion.[4] The Anthem/Cigna combination would create the largest U.S. health insurer, with $115 billion in annual revenue and 53 million members—about 20 percent of Americans.[5]

CVS Health recently purchased the pharmacy and clinic business of Target for about $1.9 billion, adding 1,672 retail pharmacies and 79 retail clinics,[6] bringing the number of CVS MinuteClinic locations to more than 1,100, and building on CVS's 50 percent retail clinic market share and 27 million patient visits.[7] *The New York Times* called CVS "arguably the country's biggest health care company, bigger than the drug makers and wholesalers, and bigger than the insurers."[8]

Within just over a year, Roche, the world's largest biotech company, made six acquisitions and investments in genomics companies: GeneWEAVE, Kapa Biosystems, Genia Technologies, Bina Technologies, Signature Diagnostics, and Foundation Medicine.[9] Roche's 2015 revenues were more than $48 billion, and it has more than 90,000 employees.[10]

These are the kinds of companies that will be influencing and controlling healthcare in the future: *Big* data companies looking to narrow the use of high-intensity services through predictive analytics and personal health monitoring. *Big* pharmacies trying to gain more influence on the provision of low-intensity healthcare. *Big* insurers looking to position themselves as the organizers of care. And *big* drug companies looking to change the very nature of care with new genomic technologies. To stay in the healthcare game, a company needs *big* operations, *big* intellectual capital, *big* cash flow, and the ability to raise *big* capital.

At the broadest level, hospitals have two choices: stick to tradition and see their share of the healthcare pie and relevance shrink, or figure out a way to get big enough to compete in a much larger and more taxing arena.

Enter the FTC

The FTC appears determined to keep hospitals in the smallest box possible. Ignoring the changing nature of healthcare described above, the FTC applies an antiquated, price-focused view of competition, while other federal agencies take a relatively hands-off approach as hospitals' new competitors grow.

In recent months, the FTC has picked up the pace of challenges to hospital mergers and acquisitions. Within six weeks, the FTC challenged a proposed merger between Advocate Health Care Network and NorthShore University Health System in the Chicago area;[11] a proposed merger between Penn State Hershey Medical Center and PinnacleHealth System in the Harrisburg, Pennsylvania area;[12] and a proposed acquisition by Cabell Huntington Hospital of St. Mary's Medical Center in Huntington, West Virginia.[13]

In these cases and others, the FTC's challenges rest on the assumptions that these health system combinations will reduce competition, giving hospitals power to charge higher prices. Further, the FTC says that these combinations will not improve quality and efficiency.

These contentions are flawed. The FTC tends to define service areas narrowly, heightening the appearance of potential anti-competitive effects.[14] The FTC assumes a pricing power that even large healthcare organizations don't have in the face of larger and growing insurers.[15] And the enhanced capabilities for capacity management and care coordination that these hospital mergers facilitate are key to the federal government's own policies aimed at achieving improved quality and efficiency of both inpatient and outpatient services.

Far more problematic is the narrowness of the FTC's view of consolidation. By seeing hospital mergers primarily through the lens of pricing acute-care services, the FTC misses the enormity of change in healthcare and the critical importance of encouraging the not-for-profit provider community to be an essential part of that change. Hospitals will be pushed out of the market by IBM, the large insurers, CVS, Walgreens, and others unless they are big enough to compete both through traditional services and by expanding in many, may new directions.

Given current FTC policies and procedures, hospitals' battle for relevance is being lost before it can even be fought.

The Role of Consolidation for Hospitals

Government policymakers and market forces have converged on population health management as the starting line for our nation's efforts to reduce healthcare costs, improve care quality, and reduce fragmentation. Without scale and size, the vast majority of hospitals and health systems will be unable to develop the network size and breadth, talent, and technology to reach this starting line.

However, companies like IBM, CVS, and others are already moving aggressively beyond population health management, toward a new healthcare ecosystem built on sophisticated interactions among science, technology, scale, and service. Already, hospitals' competitors are more likely to be these multi-billion-dollar companies than another hospital down the street.

Despite the increasing pace of hospital and health system mergers in the last 10 years, very few existing provider organizations have the size to be a meaningful player in this environment. Any growth that hospitals have been able to achieve pales in comparison with the size of existing and emerging industry giants.

Hospitals are critical to the effectiveness of healthcare in America. Their pervasiveness, community focus, expertise in high-intensity services, and mission to stay by the sides of their patients across all levels of health and stages of life make hospitals central to a high-functioning national healthcare system. However, without the ability to get big, hospitals will find that they are at a competitive disadvantage in the emerging healthcare ecosystem.

The FTC clearly has a mandate and a job to do, but this set of problems should be thought about differently.

References

1   Japsen, B.: "IBM Watson to Buy Truven Health for $2.6 Billion, Bolsters Data Cloud." *Forbes,* Feb. 18, 2016.

2   Banerjee, A., Pierson, R. "Anthem to Buy Cigna, Creating Biggest U.S. Health Insurer." Reuters, July 24, 2015.

3   Bray, C., Abelson, R. "Aetna Agrees to Acquire Humana for $37 Billion in Cash and Stock." *The New York Times*, Jul. 3, 2015.

4   Tracer, Z.: "Centene to Buy Health Net in $6.3 Billion Health-Care Deal." *Bloomberg Business*, Jul. 2, 2015.

5   Terhune, C.: "Anthem to Buy Cigna for $54 Billion, Creating Nation's Largest Insurer." *Los Angeles Times,* Jul. 24, 2015.

6   "CVS Health and Target Announce Completed Acquisition of Target's Pharmacy and Clinic Businesses." CVS Health, press release, Dec. 16, 2015.

7   "CVS Health at a Glance," accessed Feb. 19, 2016; Bachrach, D., et al.: *Building a Culture Of Health: The Value Proposition of Retail Clinics*. Robert Wood Johnson Foundation, Manatt, Apr. 2015.

8   Tabuchi, H.: "How CVS Quit Smoking and Grew into a Health Care Giant." *The New York Times,* Jul. 11, 2015.

9   Smith, C.: "Roche Acquisitions Continue." *Front Line Genomics*, Aug. 20 2015.

10   *Annual Report 2015*, Roche, 2015.

11   Federal Trade Commission, Docket No. 9369, Complaint, Dec. 17, 2015.

12   Federal Trade Commission, Docket No. 9368, Complaint, Dec. 7, 2015.

13   Federal Trade Commission, Docket No. 9366, Complaint, Nov. 5, 2015.

14   Fischer, A.M., Marx, D.: "FTC Challenges Chicago-Area Health System Combination." McDermott Will & Emery, Dec. 23, 2015.

15   Sachdev, A.: "NorthShore CEO Ready to Fight Regulators—and He's Been There Before." *Chicago Tribune,* Jan. 8, 2016.

Innovation

More Thoughts About Artificial Intelligence

MARCH 26, 2024

With Amanda Steele, Managing Director, Kaufman Hall, and Bharat Sundaram, President, Data and Digital, Vizient

These days one can't talk enough or learn enough about artificial intelligence. It's either the fast-coming evil empire or the potential savior of modern civilization. The truth will likely, as always, be somewhere in between. In that regard, we would like to accomplish the following with this blog:

1. Recommend an essential new article that provides a most exceptional and nuanced explanation of AI;

2. Comment on a remarkable recent report that provides an insight to the potential power of AI; and

3. Raise and discuss a number of developing AI-based strategic issues for hospital and health systems.

Part I: Jaron Lanier

Jaron Lanier holds the somewhat baffling title at Microsoft of "Prime Unifying Scientist." Lanier is a computer scientist, a futurist, and a composer of contemporary classical music. He is also considered one of the founders of virtual reality.

On March 1, 2024, Lanier published an article in *The New Yorker* magazine entitled "How to Picture A.I."[1] To say the very least, this is a brilliant article; brilliantly constructed and brilliantly written. If you haven't been able to entirely grasp AI from previous readings, this article will solve that problem. As a colleague of mine said, "Lanier does a remarkable job of explaining to the reader what AI is and what terms like deep learning and generative AI mean functionally." Lanier comments that "if we can't understand how a technology works, we risk succumbing to magical thinking." This is a powerful observation for organizational executives who must decide when to use AI technologies and when not to.

Lanier organizes his article into four steps, which he calls a "human- centered cartoon," and the four conceptual steps are Trees, The Magic Forest, Forest Products, and Phantom Trees. This all seems mysterious, but Lanier's explanatory powers are rather remarkable. We can't recommend this article highly enough. It is mandatory reading for executive teams throughout provider healthcare.

Part II: The Klarna Announcement

Klarna is a Sweden-based fintech company that operates in the "buy-now-pay-later" space. According to a March 4th *Forbes* article, Klarna maintained in a recent press release that an AI assistant created by ChatGPT is now handling "the workload of 700 full-time staff members."[2] Klarna further represented that the AI algorithm is managing two-thirds of customer service chats—2.3 million conversations—in an extraordinary 23 markets and 35 languages. Further, repeat inquiries from customers have decreased by 25% and the average conversation time was reduced from 11 minutes to 2 minutes. With all of this, Klarna reduced its head count in 2023 by 25% and expects an increase in profitability of $40 million.

No matter where your first thoughts about the power and impact of AI have taken you operationally—the Klarna numbers are startling. Your first reaction might be the same as ours: What if these results are multiplied over 1000s of companies worldwide? The impact on workforce and profitability might be incalculable.

Your second thought, however, might be that despite the Klarna report, the ongoing impact of AI might be much more nuanced and complicated. For example, the impact of AI on workforce could be dramatically different in developing economies versus the impact in highly developed economies like the United States or Western Europe. The AI impact could be accelerated in areas characterized by workforce shortages or, in fact, AI might actually be a job creator rather than a job destroyer. Understanding the actual AI trends will likely be most important to guiding operational AI decisions within your own organization. The Klarna report, and other reports to come, certainly should gain and keep the attention of healthcare executives.

Part III: Fast Developing AI Strategic Issues

AI might be a "tool," but it may be unlike any "tool" we have seen before. And, therefore, it very likely will drive organizational strategies in entirely new and different ways. This brings forward an entire series of relevant corporate questions:

1. Is AI an "enabler" or a "strategy" all by itself?

2. What if AI is much more than a "tool"? What if accelerating technology moves AI to more of a "creature" status (Lanier's term) with anthropomorphic characteristics?

3. If AI is more of a "tool" for the foreseeable future, how is that going to work if you install those "tools" on top of already poorly performing hospital processes?

4. What is the creative vision necessary to combine AI with existing in-place strategies that might actually define a new provider-based value proposition accompanied by a transformative care delivery system?

5. Finally, and obviously, what is the probable impact on resource requirements, level of investment, and organizational readiness?

And the last thought for now is around the issue of AI traceability. Technically, traceability is a human readable explanation of what inputs and algorithms an AI model used to determine its outputs. Traceability is over time going to be a big deal generally in artificial intelligence, but it will be a much bigger deal in the healthcare vertical, especially as it relates to the use of AI within clinical care, particularly how any AI model makes recommendations on diagnoses and treatment. There have been cases where a large language model has produced well-structured and seemingly believable answers to medical questions citing scientific papers and medical journals that don't, in fact, exist. This AI algorithm characteristic is called "hallucination," and it can generate convincing but false content. As Lanier points out in his article, tracing the specific "breadcrumbs" used to develop AI recommendations has not yet been applied in practice. Given the scale of these models (Open AI's Chat GPT-4 model may have over a trillion parameters), it is unclear when and how this required traceability will be possible.

No doubt artificial intelligence is endlessly fascinating, totally exciting, and absolutely worrisome. Our advice—read, learn, and experiment. Begin with AI cases and models where the risks and consequences of error can be anticipated and managed. Best of luck in this brave new world.

References

1   Lanier, J.: "How to Picture A.I." *The New Yorker*, Mar. 1, 2024.
2   Kelly, J.: "Klarna's AI Assistant Is Doing The Job Of 700 Workers, Company Says." *Forbes.* Mar 4, 2024.

So Much to Worry About

DECEMBER 20, 2023

I f you are a hospital executive—and if you are reading this, you probably are—then you have no shortage of worries. The worry list is long:

- Trying to control expenses.
- Dealing with declining revenue, especially when considered on an after-inflation basis.
- Struggling with ongoing staffing issues that have no immediate solutions.
- Solving the longstanding problem of patient access to appointments and service.

And the list could go on and on.

But maybe the biggest concern is one that is not on many worry lists: the remarkable development of artificial intelligence (AI) and how AI is relentlessly pushing into business practice generally and into healthcare more specifically. While the long-term worry is how your hospital will carefully and properly adopt AI inside the business and clinical parts of your organization, the more immediate and short-term worry is whether you, as an executive, understand AI in a way that you can be ultimately useful to your organization.

Full disclosure: I can't help here much. For me, AI is a pretty big black box. But when I confront this kind of business problem I start reading and learning. One of the most useful AI articles I have come across is "The Optimists: The Full Story of

Microsoft's Relationship with OpenAI," which was published in the December 1, 2023, issue of *The New Yorker* magazine.[1] The article was written by Charles Duhigg, a former winner of the Pulitzer Prize.

I am hoping that for your own professional development you will read the Duhigg article, but just in case, here are the highlights:

- Microsoft has reportedly invested $13 billion in the for-profit arm of OpenAI.
- Using OpenAI technology, Microsoft has built a series of AI assistants into Word, Outlook, and PowerPoint. These AI assistants are now known as Office Copilots.
- Knowledgeable commentators say these Microsoft applications are only moderately sophisticated but, honestly, they seem rather remarkable to me. Here are some of Duhiggs's examples of requests Office Copilot users can make:
  - "Tell me the pros and cons of each plan described on that video call."
  - "What's the most profitable product in these twenty spreadsheets?"
- How about writing projects? Duhigg notes that the Office Copilot can:
  - Create a financial narrative of the past decade based on a company's last ten executive summaries.
  - Turn a memo into a PowerPoint.
  - Compile a to-do list for Teams video attendees, in multiple languages, after listening in on a meeting.

- Later in the article Duhigg details the functionality of the Word Copilot:
  - "You can ask it to reduce a five-page document to ten bullet points…[o]r…it can take the ten bullet points and transform them into a five-page document."
  - It can write a memo based on previous emails you have written.
  - "You can ask, 'Did I forget to include anything that usually appears in a contract like this?,' and the Copilot will review your previous contracts."

Duhigg reports that Microsoft previously acquired a company called GitHub. GitHub is "a website where users shared code and collaborated on software." Microsoft operates GitHub as an independent division. GitHub has been a very big success and is used by software engineers and, in a short period of time, has grown to over 100 million users.

OpenAI created an artificial intelligence tool that autocompletes software code. Despite reservations at Microsoft, GitHub President Nat Friedman decided to release the GitHub Copilot autocomplete tool. The result has been $100 million in revenue to GitHub in less than a year.

At the end of the article, Duhigg notes that these early AI business applications are both "impressive and banal." Banal because they don't yet live up to the sci-fi predictions for AI and its long-term impact on society.

Honestly, I don't see it that way. This OpenAI/Microsoft collaboration is only scratching the surface and its potential uses are already endless, waiting to be invented by 100s of millions of users all over the world, including in healthcare. From my seat, the sky is the limit here. Almost anything seems possible.

I hope this summary of Mr. Duhigg's exceptional article proves useful and advances your awareness of AI's aggressive and rapid move into day-to-day business—here, through many of the Microsoft productivity programs that every one of us uses every day. In any case, I recommend that you read Duhigg's entire article. It is most certainly worth your time.

References

1 Duhigg, C.: "The Inside Story of Microsoft's Partnership with OpenAI." *The New Yorker*, Dec. 1, 2023.

AI, Breast Cancer, and a New Mindset for Healthcare

FEBRUARY 2, 2022

A recent feature in *The Washington Post* speaks volumes about both the future of healthcare and the potential willingness of society and the healthcare establishment to embrace that future.[1]

Regina Barzilay is an artificial-intelligence researcher at the Massachusetts Institute of Technology and a breast cancer survivor. During the past seven years, Barzilay put her AI experience to work in developing a new machine-learning tool for early detection of breast cancer.

"Learning" is the key word here. AI takes huge data sets and uses algorithms that, over time, learn from patterns in the data. In this case, Barzilay and her team set out to teach the machine-learning tool to see the relationships between the rich data shown in a mammogram—much of it not currently used for diagnosis—and the chances of an individual developing breast cancer.

After using 200,000 mammograms to "teach" Barzilay's tool, named Mirai, the team conducted a study that showed Mirai was capable of predicting three-quarters of occurrences of breast cancer up to five years before they happened, a 22% improvement over the currently used statistical model, which determines risk based on age, family history, and other factors.

The positive implications for health and healthcare are enormous. Mirai—which is open source and so can potentially be used and improved by multiple researchers and providers—could refine breast cancer screenings to better focus on individuals with high risk. Mirai also could reduce the racial bias that exists in current models for predicting breast cancer, which occurs at a significantly higher rate among women of color.

Three years before her breast cancer diagnosis, Barzilay had a mammogram that indicated "everything was fine." Years later, out of curiosity, Barzilay fed this mammogram into Mirai. The tool told Barzilay that at the time she had been at high risk for breast cancer.

But what the tool could not do is tell Barzilay *why* she was at high risk for cancer.

AI is confounding. It goes against the deep instinct we all have to know why things happen. Understanding causal relationships is at the heart of all intellectual inquiry—certainly it is central to the scientific method and to medicine.

Yet AI forces us into a place where *explicable* causal relationships have been replaced by *inexplicable* causal relationships.

Consider how medicine works now. A physician orders tests for a patient—blood work, radiology images, etc. The physician and patient sit down and go over the results of those tests, and the physician says, "Based on these results, this is the scientifically determined effective course of treatment."

With AI, the discussion would be very different. Instead it would be something like this: "The algorithm tells us that you are at high risk for developing breast cancer, but we can't tell you what the algorithm actually sees or why it thinks you are at risk, but we do know that the algorithm is correct a high percentage of the time."

That is a very different conversation. And for many providers and patients, it may be a very uncomfortable conversation. If COVID has taught us anything, it's the importance of societal trust in science. However, that trust may be strained if we cannot explain why a certain condition is being forecast and why a particular course of care is being recommended. For consumers, AI could exacerbate a skepticism about expertise that is already dangerously high in this country. For healthcare professionals—radiologists in particular—AI in medicine may appear to fly in the face of their professional training while disrupting their professional roles.

Cornell mathematician Steven Strogatz articulated this dilemma in a *New York Times* essay about artificial intelligence's success in playing chess: "What is frustrating about machine learning," Strogatz wrote, "is that the algorithms can't articulate what they're thinking. We don't know why they work, so we don't know if they can be trusted."[2]

In chess, this lack of trust may be frustrating, but in healthcare it could be an impediment to adoption and therefore to the best possible healthcare outcomes, including the saving of lives.

This lack of trust was, perhaps, what informed the reaction of traditional healthcare provider organizations when Barzilay first approached them seven years ago to supply mammograms to assist with developing her AI tool.

Most hospitals turned her away, saying, according the *Washington Post* article, that breast cancer had been treated for years without AI. Barzilay recalled, "They acted like I was trying to sell snow to an Eskimo."

Barzilay's own care provider, Massachusetts General Hospital, eventually agreed to help, and supplied the mammograms for initial development of the tool. Since then, Barzilay has made great progress, with Novant and Emory in the U.S. and health systems in Israel, Sweden, Taiwan, and Brazil participating in the research to show the tool's capabilities.[3]

Despite the eventual increase in participation in this project, and despite many health systems' own initiatives in artificial intelligence and precision medicine, the reaction that Barzilay met with is concerning when viewed in a broader context.

The future of healthcare is moving rapidly beyond the legacy intellectual and attitudinal framework. Hospitals and health systems find themselves needing to operate outside their traditional span of responsibility, taking on vast challenges like health equity and public health. Hospitals also need to operate on a macroeconomic platform redefined by big tech companies, a platform of big data, ideas, resources, scale, and strategic aggressiveness.

In many ways, the example of Regina Barzilay and her AI tool for early detection of breast cancer highlights what hospitals are facing on multiple levels. AI is a new idea, one that even data experts don't fully understand. It requires big data, expertise, and resources. And it requires a new view of the role of healthcare in improving health and preventing disease.

The foundations for success in this environment are curiosity and openness: curiosity about what benefits may come from new concepts, and openness to active participation in bringing those concepts to practical fruition.

When Barzilay first asked health systems to help in her development of a new approach to breast cancer diagnosis, she encountered general unwillingness. The good news is that over time, this mindset was replaced by curiosity about the possibilities and openness to assist.

That is exactly the shift in mindset that will be needed on a large scale as we confront the very new set of challenges and the very new environment that healthcare professionals find themselves facing today.

References

1   Zeitchik, S.: "Is Artificial Intelligence About to Transform the Mammogram?" *Washington Post*, Dec. 21, 2021.

2   Strogatz, S.: "One Giant Step for a Chess-Playing Machine." *The New York Times*, Dec. 26, 2018.

3   Yala, A., et al: "Multi-Institutional Validation of a Mammography-Based Breast Cancer Risk Model." *Journal of Clinical Oncology*, 40(16), Nov. 12, 2021.

How Telehealth Could Fail

DECEMBER 24, 2020

After several years of research and development, the automated teller machine made its first appearance in 1967 at a branch of London's Barclay's Bank.[1] Two years later, the first U.S. ATM was installed at a branch of the Chemical Bank on Long Island.

However, ATMs remained a minimally used curiosity until one bank took a risk and external forces took control. In 1977, Citibank made a big bet on ATMs. (Do any of you New Yorkers remember the slogan, "The Citi that never sleeps"?) Then in January of 1978, New York City was hit with a snowstorm that closed bank branches for days, leading to a double-digit increase in ATM use. After that, other banks hurried to invest in the new technology. Over the next several decades, ATMs proliferated, climbing to a peak of 2 million worldwide.

Despite the popularity of ATMs, remote banking would have fallen far short of its potential if progress had stopped there. Today's smartphone-enabled banking capabilities—budgeting, fraud protection, loan application, funds transfer, and on and on—leave ATMs in the dust when it comes to access, convenience, and tools.

In March of 2020, healthcare was in roughly the same place with telehealth as banks were in 1977 with ATMs. After years of research and development, telehealth was on the radar of most healthcare provider organizations, but relatively few had extensively deployed the technology. In 2019, Kaufman Hall's State of

Consumerism report found that only 20% of organizations had widely available video visits.[2]

Then came COVID-19, and with it a 154% increase in telehealth use at the peak of the pandemic's first wave.[3] Organizations routinely reported accelerating their telehealth plans by years in order to accommodate the demand from patients not able to see providers in person.

However, as with ATMs and banking, telehealth will be a failure if it goes no further than today's video visits and other routine features.

Siddhartha Mukherjee, MD, DPhil, Pulitzer Prize-winning author, and renowned virologist and cancer researcher, made this point forcefully in a presentation at Kaufman Hall's Healthcare Leadership Conference last month. Mukherjee noted, first, that too often video visits are isolated encounters rather than part of a care plan with measurable goals and steps. Worse still, Mukherjee said, is when a video visit concludes simply by scheduling an in-person visit, essentially making the health system bear the cost of two visits instead of one.

But, Mukherjee said, the true failure would be if telehealth does not take advantage of the clinical and cost breakthroughs possible through increasingly advanced technology leading to a fully integrated digital health platform.

COVID has been to telehealth what the 1978 New York City blizzard was to ATMs. For banking, ATMs were just a first step in greater efficiency, convenience, and use of technology. The responsibility of healthcare providers now is to keep telehealth momentum going. That means continuing to promote telehealth to consumers and clinicians. It means improving the execution and efficiency of current practices. It means advocating for fair payment for telehealth services. And most of all, it means developing, investing in, partnering for, and promulgating sophisticated new digital technology that can bring about major advances in outcomes, convenience, and affordability.

COVID has had a devastating impact on the U.S. healthcare system, and we don't yet know the intensity or duration of that impact. One positive glimmer that has come from COVID is the rapid adoption of telehealth. It is up to healthcare provider organizations to turn that glimmer into the bright light of progress. To fail in that effort would be to add yet another blow to the long list that COVID has delivered.

References

1 "Automated Teller Machines." History.com, Aug. 21, 2018.

2 *2019 State of Consumerism in Healthcare The Bar Is Rising*, Kaufman Hall & Associates, 2019.

3 *Trends in the Use of Telehealth During the Emergence of the COVID-19 Pandemic — United States, January–March 2020*. Centers for Disease Control and Prevention, 2020.

Innovation Needs Entrepreneurs

APRIL 3, 2019

A recent AHA survey found that 72 percent of larger hospitals and health systems have built or are in the process of building an innovation center.[1]

Legacy healthcare organizations see innovation as a crucial path to staying relevant in a fast-changing world. Innovation has the promise to solve longstanding problems with the healthcare system, to move legacy organizations into a digital world, and discover new revenue channels as volume and payment from traditional channels soften. Adding to the momentum for innovation is the rise of competitors—from start-ups to tech giants—that have innovation in their DNA.

Structurally, hospital innovation programs range from projects or departments housed within a hospital to subsidiary companies to partnerships with tech companies. Traditionally, hospital innovation programs have focused on developing internal ideas to be used within the hospital to improve issues like operational efficiency or utilization management. In the face of new competition and rapid change, these programs increasingly develop and fund start-up companies whose goal is to sell new products to new markets.

As the need for innovation intensifies, so does the need for a new orientation toward innovation. The capabilities, culture, and mission that support ongoing operations of a legacy healthcare organization are not those that drive successful innovation. In order for innovation to generate ideas that become commercial successes, it must be backed by an entrepreneurial culture with characteristics that are different from—and even antithetical to—the characteristics of legacy organizations.

8 Characteristics of Entrepreneurial Organizations

An innovation center cannot be simply an add-on to the ongoing operations of a legacy healthcare organization. It must be rooted in a culture of entrepreneurialism, led by individuals who demonstrate eight critical characteristics.

Have really good ideas. The foundation of a successful entrepreneur are breakthrough ideas. Such ideas are transformational. They offer solutions to needs that may not even be recognized. They are the product of thinking differently about how important tasks can be done and how important goals can be achieved. They open up new demand from the largest possible markets.

Work hard in a different way. Legacy healthcare organizations are full of hard workers. But entrepreneurial organizations need people who work hard in a different way. In legacy organizations, people work hard at doing their best within existing workflows. In entrepreneurial organizations, people work hard at disrupting those workflows in the search for something better. They will be relentless in asking questions, conceptualizing solutions, and making them successful.

Tolerate risk. Healthcare organizations have a reputation of being averse to risk. Healthcare organizations are not alone in this. All companies are subject to organizational forces and natural biases that make their leaders reluctant to take on risk. In contrast, innovation and entrepreneurialism are by definition about taking risks. They require leaders who can recognize these forces and biases and move beyond them.

Persevere. In part because legacy healthcare organizations tend to avoid risk, they have little experience with meeting unexpected problems or confronting failure. Instead, they develop processes and protocols that are designed to avoid failure. Surgical procedures, for example, can't go bad because a surgeon wants to go down an unknown path that may or may not produce a better outcome for the patient. Entrepreneurial organizations encounter obstacles and outright failures regularly. They need to develop perseverance as a business emotion that enables them to get over obstacles and failures and keep going. In 2014, when Amazon's introduction of the Fire smartphone failed, *Fortune* magazine reported that the company "is now left scrambling, and it's unclear whether it can recover from its flop."[2] Amazon persevered, recovered fully, and continues to grow.

Feel a sense of urgency. Because hospitals want to be careful, methodical, and tactical, they don't want to rush. Entrepreneurial organizations face forces that push them in the opposite direction. These forces have grown only stronger in the internet economy. In a phenomenon that has been called "big-bang disruption," innovation can now "come out of nowhere and instantly be everywhere."[3] Being first to market with a new idea is more important than ever. Adding to this pressure is the fact that entrepreneurial organizations typically make their run at innovation with limited funds. They have neither time nor money to waste.

Integrate disassociated ideas. Netflix did not invent the technology for streaming video. It realized that existing video compression technology could be deployed to deliver movies through lines that internet service providers had already run to consumers' homes—and it continues to refine this strategy as it expands internationally across varying digital infrastructures.[4] Uber combined existing geolocation, texting, and digital payment technologies to transform an untapped supply of independent drivers into a worldwide fleet that has disrupted the taxi business and threatens legacy auto makers as well.[5] An entrepreneur takes two ideas that are disassociated and puts them together, creating a new idea and a new product or service for sale.

Develop strategic intuition. Legacy healthcare organizations and entrepreneurs share a commitment to numbers and data. But entrepreneurs are dealing with the new. They can't know in advance if their innovations will become game changers, so they must be willing to beyond data and market research and trust their intuition. When Steve Jobs introduced the iPhone, predicting that it would be a "revolutionary product…that changes everything," he was met with skepticism from many. Microsoft's then-CEO Steve Ballmer said, "There's no chance the iPhone is going to get any significant market share." Jobs knew better, with an innovation that did indeed change the world.[6]

Obsess over sales. Legacy hospitals are concerned with market share, but their focus is on referrals: How can we get clinicians to bring their cases to us? Entrepreneurs are starting with an idea that needs to be sold to bring in revenue that covers expenses and allows further growth. First, they need to convince people to try their idea, and then to pay money for it. Because innovations are new, consumers will not have heard of them, and may not even understand why they might need them. Entrepreneurial organizations need people who not only are excited by the innovation, but also obsessed with bringing it to the attention of others.

Creating an Entrepreneurial Culture
Because the characteristics of entrepreneurial organizations can differ so much from the characteristics of legacy hospitals and health

systems, healthcare organizations that are thinking about adding an innovation vertical face some challenges.

First, they should be willing to make the work of the innovation center completely separate from the work of the legacy organization. Without this separation, the work of innovation will too easily be set aside in favor of work that sustains a current business model.

Second, they should understand that even though innovations may seriously disrupt the legacy organization's current business models, innovators need free rein to pursue disruption. If they don't do it, there are others who will.

Third, and most important, they must be sure that the capabilities of those who are given the task of pursuing innovation are compatible with the characteristics of entrepreneurial organizations. Some of these capabilities may be found within the legacy organization. More often, the legacy organization will need to look beyond its existing talent if it wants to create an entrepreneurial culture that will drive innovations from ideas to commercial success.

References

1 "Survey: Hospital CEOs See Digital Innovation as Critical, But Significant Roadblocks Remain." AVIA, press release, Sept. 21, 2017.

2 Mangalinden, J.P.: "Why Amazon's Fire Phone Failed." *Fortune*, Sept. 29, 2014.

3 Downes, L., Nunes, P.: "Big-Bang Disruption." *Harvard Business Review*, Mar. 2013.

4 Velazco, C.: "Netflix Learned How to Stream Good Video on Bad Connections." Engadget, Mar. 1, 2017.

5 Abrosymova, K.: "Building an App Like Uber: What Is the Uber App Made From?" Medium, May 22, 2014.

6 Vena, D.: "12 Years Ago Steve Jobs Introduced the iPhone, and Everything Changed." The Motley Fool, Apr. 15, 2019.

Transforming the Patient Experience: One Patient's Story

JANUARY 12, 2016

A colleague of mine I'll call Mary is fighting Stage IIIC ovarian cancer. Recently, Mary came down with a bad stomach infection. She reached an on-call physician, who told her to go to the ER, where she would be admitted to the hospital.

When Mary arrived at the ER, she found 50 patients waiting to be seen. She took her place in the queue. Eventually, she was screened by ER staff, who directed her to wait to be evaluated by a physician, despite the fact that the on-call physician had already determined to admit her to the hospital.

Almost three hours after arrival at the ER, Mary still hadn't been seen by a physician, much less admitted. She reached the on-call physician and asked if the process could be accelerated. The physician promised to try. Finally, four hours after arriving at the ER for what should have been essentially a routine transaction, Mary was admitted to her room.

The Importance of Coordination

Patients experience healthcare not as discrete encounters, or as a linear progression along a continuum, but as a complex system of interdependent structures, processes, behaviors, and outcomes.

As healthcare systems grow larger, encompass more facilities, and cover a greater span of the care continuum, complexity increases and coordination gets harder.

The emerging value-based payment system is increasing the importance of coordination while changing its nature. Coordination now requires not just seamless execution of individual episodes of care, but continuous coordination in order to maintain health over time, avoid unnecessary hospitalization, and ensure effective transitions from one care setting to another.

In addition, consumers have higher expectations for service delivery, driven both by their greater financial responsibility for healthcare costs and by sky-high levels of service from companies such as Amazon and Nordstrom.

Some nontraditional healthcare competitors are making care coordination a core component of their value proposition, touting the use of dedicated care navigators and ready access to providers by phone, email, and text.

To remain relevant, legacy healthcare organizations must get coordination right.

Another Example

Mary had scheduled the lab tests that were required for her chemo treatment in conjunction with placement of the chest port so that she didn't need a separate appointment for the tests. She coordinated this arrangement with her oncology team, alerted her chemo team, and notified the facility where the port procedure would be done. In addition, she reiterated the need for lab tests during each of four calls she received confirming her port procedure.

When she arrived for the port procedure, she reminded the nurse about the tests that were needed for the next day's chemo.

The nurse checked the medical record and said that she did not have any orders for lab tests.

My colleague asked the nurse to contact the chemo team. The nurse reached someone who confirmed the need for tests, but told the nurse that one of the tests was not necessary.

After the port procedure, my colleague called the location where the chemo would take place, and the person on the phone confirmed that they had all the tests needed. However, the next morning the chemo facility called to say that the omitted test was, in fact, necessary. After devoting so much time and energy to avoid having to schedule tests the morning before chemo, my colleague still had to arrive early to have the omitted test done.

"Chemo or No Chemo, I'm Happy to Help"

After hearing about these experiences, I arranged for Mary to speak with a senior executive at the hospital. Mary returned from the meeting energized.

Mary began her discussion with the executive by emphasizing that the hospital staff consistently tried to help her and to do the right thing. Then she told her story—about the wait in the ER and the miscommunication over lab tests, along with the challenges of reaching the right person by phone, confusion over having multiple contacts, and difficulty absorbing the overwhelming amount of information provided. Mary offered suggestions for improvement in each of these areas.

The executive listened carefully and took extensive notes throughout. He discussed each situation seriously and knowledgably. In some cases, the problems were a surprise; in others they were known. In some cases, the executive promised to investigate; in others, he noted that improvements were underway. He was frank about the time involved in making changes in a complex and growing organization. Throughout, he was grateful for the information, unstinting in his attention, and concerned about my colleague's health.

"He really is one of the good ones," Mary reported. "I'd like to do more. Chemo or no chemo, I'm happy to help."

Transforming the Patient Experience

I was quite moved by this story.

Illness in general and cancer specifically can be frightening, exhausting, and disheartening. Just getting through each day can be a major struggle. For Mary, the opportunity to transform her personal struggle into help for others in similar circumstances was a form of renewal.

On many days, the pace and complexity of running a hospital can be overwhelming. Emails must be answered, meetings can't be missed, and the pile of documents needing review grows. In this case, the hospital executive saw an opportunity to step off the daily treadmill and get to the core of the hospital's mission: helping patients.

In an era of consumerism, delivering an excellent patient experience day-in and day-out is essential for success. Improving that experience must start with an understanding of the patient's perspective. Getting that perspective requires active listening—seeking out patients' insights informally and in regular, structured conversations. Then, the learnings must be translated into constant and consequential improvements in the factors that mean the most to patients.

As Mary's story illustrates, listening to patients can bring truly remarkable benefits. It can highlight process problems that the hospital hadn't recognized. It can create urgency, energy, and enthusiasm for improvement. It can build patient loyalty. It can create a more collaborative relationship between patients and the hospital. Also, by showing patients that their insights are valued, listening can give patients a renewed sense of purpose and worth at an otherwise distressing time in their lives.

Listening is helping.

About the Author

As Kaufman Hall's Managing Director and one of the firm's founding partners, Ken Kaufman has provided the nation's top healthcare leaders with expert counsel and guidance since 1976. He is recognized as a leading authority on healthcare macro trends, with his areas of expertise spanning strategy, finance, financial and capital planning, and mergers, acquisitions, and partnerships.

Ken offers deep insights on the economic, technological, and competitive forces undermining healthcare's traditional business model. He has delivered almost 600 speeches and is the author of eight books, including *Fast and Furious: Observations on Healthcare's Transformation.*

Ken received his M.B.A., with a concentration in Hospital Administration, from the University of Chicago.

Ken received the 2019 Richard L. Clarke Board of Directors Award from the Healthcare Financial Management Association for lifetime contribution to healthcare, the only consultant to receive this recognition. In 2024, he received the American Hospital Association's Award of Honor, which is given to individuals or organizations in recognition of exemplary contributions to the health and well-being of our nation through leadership on major health policy or social initiatives.

References

"10 Essential Public Health Services." Centers for Disease Control and Prevention, May 15, 2024.

"192 Rural Hospital Closures and Conversions since January 2005." University of North Carolina Cecil G. Sheps Center for Health Services Research, accessed Feb. 28, 2019..

2017 State of Consumerism in Healthcare, Kaufman Hall & Associates, 2017.

2018 Broadband Deployment Report. Federal Communications Commission, Feb. 2, 2018.

2019 State of Consumerism in Healthcare The Bar Is Rising, Kaufman Hall & Associates, 2019.

Abelson, R., Hsu, T.: "Amazon, Berkshire Hathaway and JPMorgan Name C.E.O. for Health Initiative." *The New York Times*, Jun. 20, 2018.

"About CVS Health." CVS Health.

"About Us." AnyLabTestNow.

Abrosymova, K.: "Building an App Like Uber: What Is the Uber App Made From?" Medium, May 22, 2014.

Annual Report 2015, Roche, 2015.

"Advocate Aurora Health raises minimum wage to $18/hour." Advocate Health Care, press release, Nov. 11, 2021.

"Alexa, What's for Dinner Tonight?" Morgan Stanley, Jul. 21, 2017.

"An Announcement from Prevea Health and Aaron Rodgers Regarding Their Partnership." Prevea Health, Jul. 8, 2022.

"Automated Teller Machines." History.com, Aug. 21, 2018.

Bagley, N.: "Medicine as a Public Calling," *Michigan Law Review*, 114(1), 2015.

Ball, J.: "Inside Oil Giant Shell's Race to Remake Itself for a Low-Price World." *Fortune*, Jan. 24, 2018.

Banerjee, A., Pierson, R. "Anthem to Buy Cigna, Creating Biggest U.S. Health Insurer." Reuters, July 24, 2015.

Barkholz, D.: "Kaiser Permanente Chief Says Members are Flocking to Virtual Visits." *Modern Healthcare*, Apr. 21, 2017.

Bates, M., Andersen, J.: "Renters or Owners: Real Estate and Physician Affiliation." Kaufman Hall, Sept. 23, 2021.

Bates, M., Swanson, E.: *Physician Flash Report: Q1 2023*. Kaufman, Hall & Associates, May 3, 2023.

Beer, J.: "How Domino's Became a Tech Company." *Fast Company*, May 22, 2014.

Belson, K., Vrentas, J.: "Brian Flores Sues N.F.L., Claiming Bias in Coaching Search." *The New York Times*, Feb. 1, 2022.

Benjamins, M.R., De Maio, F.G. (eds.): *Unequal Cities: Structural Racism and the Death Gap in America's Largest Cities*. Hopkins Press, 2021.

Black Representation in the C-Suite, The Chartis Group, May 25, 2021.

Boot, M.: "When Did Dr. Aaron Rodgers, QB, Acquire a PhD in Epidemiology?" *Washington Post*, Nov. 8, 2021.

Bray, C., Abelson, R. "Aetna Agrees to Acquire Humana for $37 Billion in Cash and Stock." *The New York Times*, Jul. 3, 2015.

Brennan, C.: "State Farm Stands by Aaron Rodgers After His Vaccine Comments: 'Respect His Right' to Have His Own Point of View." *USA Today*, Nov. 8, 2021.

Brooks, A.C.: *From Strength to Strength: Finding Success, Happiness, and Deep Purpose in the Second Half of Life*. Penguin Random House, 2022.

Bryant, B.: "Protect Funding for Core Local Public Health Services and Prevention Programs." National Association of Counties, Jan. 23, 2024.

Byers, J.: "Optum a Step Ahead in Vertical Integration Frenzy," *Healthcare Dive*, Apr. 12, 2018.

CAH Financial Indicators Report: Summary of Indicator Medians by State. Flex Monitoring Team, Flex Monitoring Team Data Summary Report No. 26, March 2018.

"CEO Strategic Update," Ford Motor Company, Oct. 3, 2017.

City Health Dashboard, NYU Grossman School of Medicine, Department of Population Health.

Coate, P.: "Remote Work Before, During, and After the Pandemic." National Council on Compensation Insurance, Jan. 25, 2021.

Colvin, G.: "How Intuit Reinvents Itself." *Fortune*, Oct. 20, 2017.

Commins, J.: "CVS Health Posts Strong Retail, Omnicare Outlook." *HealthLeaders*, Feb. 10, 2016.

Consumer Expenditures—2022, Bureau of Labor Statistics, Sept. 8, 2023.

Cook, I.: "Who Is Driving the Great Resignation?" *Harvard Business Review*, Sept. 15, 2021.

Coppola, D.: "Number of Amazon Prime Members in the United States as of December 2019." Statista, Jul. 14, 2023.

COVID-19 in 2021: The Potential Effect on Hospital Revenues. Kaufman Hall & Associates, 2021.

Crnkovich, P., Clarin, D., O'Riordan, J.: *2018 State of Consumerism in Healthcare: Activity in Search of Strategy*. Kaufman, Hall & Associates, 2018.

The Current State of Hospital Finances: Fall 2022 Update, Kaufman Hall & Associates, 2022.

"CVS Health and Target Announce Completed Acquisition of Target's Pharmacy and Clinic Businesses." CVS Health, press release, Dec. 16, 2015.

"CVS Health Announces Significant Expansion of HealthHUB to Deliver a Differentiated, Consumer Health Experience." CVS Health press release, Jun. 4, 2019.

"CVS Health at a Glance," accessed Feb. 19, 2016; Bachrach, D., et al.: Building a Culture Of Health: The Value Proposition of Retail Clinics. Robert Wood Johnson Foundation, Manatt, Apr. 2015.

"CVS MinuteClinic Announces the Cure for the Common Wait as it Unveils a Digital Tool Allowing Patients to Hold a Place in Line." *PRNewswire*, May 26, 2016.

De la Merced, M., Abelson, R.: "CVS to Buy Aetna for $69 Billion in a Deal that May Reshape the Health Industry." *The New York Times*, Dec. 3, 2017.

Defining Rural Population. U.S. Health Resources and Services Administration, Jan. 2024.

DePillis, L., Sherman, I.: "Amazon's Extraordinary Evolution." CNN, Oct. 4, 2018.

Designated Health Professional Shortage Areas Statistics. Bureau of Health Workforce, Health Resources and Services Administration, Mar. 4, 2019.

Diamond, D., via Twitter. Nov. 8, 2018.

Disparities. HealthyPeople.gov, 2020.

Dixon. V.: "UberEats Is Destroying Your Favorite Delivery Service," *Eater*, May 9, 2017.

Downes, L., Nunes, P.: "Big-Bang Disruption." *Harvard Business Review*, Mar. 2013.

Duhigg, C.: "The Inside Story of Microsoft's Partnership with OpenAI." *The New Yorker*, Dec. 1, 2023.

"Emergency Physicians: Anthem Blue Cross Blue Shield Policy Violates Federal Law." American College of Emergency Physicians, May 16, 2017.

Farr, C. "Apple explored buying a medical-clinic start-up as part of a bigger push into health care." CNBC, Oct. 21, 2017.

Farr, C.: "Alphabet Kicks Off a Private Two-Day Conference Dedicated to Health, Featuring AI Chief Jeff Dean and Other Leaders from All Over the Company." CNBC, Nov. 6, 2018.

Farr, C.: "Alphabet Will Track Health Data of 10,000 Volunteers to 'Create a Map of Human Health.'" CNBC, Apr. 19, 2017.

Farr, C.: "Amazon Has Plans to Open Its Own Health Clinics for Seattle Employees." CNBC, Aug. 9, 2018.

Farr, C.: "Apple Explored Buying a Medical-Clinic Start-Up as Part of a Bigger Push Into Health Care." CNBC, Oct. 21, 2017.

Farr, C.: "Apple's First Hires For Its Health Clinics Show How It's Thinking Differently About Health Care." CNBC, Aug. 2, 2018.

Federal Trade Commission, Docket No. 9366, Complaint, Nov. 5, 2015.

Federal Trade Commission, Docket No. 9368, Complaint, Dec. 7, 2015.

Federal Trade Commission, Docket No. 9369, Complaint, Dec. 17, 2015.

Filloon, W.: "How Restaurants Are Adapting to the Food Delivery Boom." *Eater*, Sept. 18, 2017.

Findlay, S.: "When You Should Go to an Urgent Care or Walk-in Health Clinic." *Consumer Reports*, May 4, 2018.

Fischer, A.M., Marx, D.: "FTC Challenges Chicago-Area Health System Combination." McDermott Will & Emery, Dec. 23, 2015.

Fisher, M.: "I Stand With Aaron Rodgers." Instagram post, Nov. 6, 2021.

Ford, R., Reber, S., Reeves, R.V.: "Race Gaps in COVID-19 Deaths Are Even Bigger Than They Appear." *The Brookings Institution*, Jun. 16, 2020.

Franck, T.: "Home Food Delivery is Surging Thanks to Ease of Online Ordering, New Study Shows." CNBC, Jul. 12, 2017.

Franck, T.: "Jamie Dimon Says Health Care Initiative with Buffett and Bezos May Start Small Like Amazon Did with Books before Expanding." CNBC, July 30, 2018.

Garfield, R., Rae, M., Claxton, G., Orgera, K.: "Double Jeopardy: Low Wage Workers at Risk for Health and Financial Implications of COVID-19." Kaiser Family Foundation, Apr. 29, 2020.

Getting Real About Inclusive Leadership, Catalyst, Nov. 21, 2019.

Gould, E., Wilson, V.: "Black Workers Face Two of the Most Lethal Preexisting Conditions for Coronavirus—Racism and Economic Inequality." Economic Policy Institute, Jun. 1, 2020.

Govindarajan, V., Ramamurti, R.: *Reverse Innovation in Health Care: How to Make Value-Based Delivery Work*. Harvard Business Review Press, 2018.

Green, D.: "Amazon's Latest Investment Hints at the Future of Alexa." *Business Insider*, Sept. 25, 2018.

Greene, J., Stevens, L.: "Wal-Mart to Vendors: Get Off Amazon's Cloud." *The Wall Street Journal*, Jun. 21, 2017.

Greene, J.: "Page 2 Readers Vote Wooden Top Coach." ESPN, Jun. 10, 2010.

Griffith, E., "Who Will Build the Next Great Car Company?" *Fortune*, Jun. 23, 2016.

Gurman, M.: "Apple Gets FDA Approval for New Watch, Touts Health Gains." *Bloomberg*, Sept. 12, 2018.

Gustafson, K.: "Amazon hints at one of Its Best-Kept Secrets: How Many Prime Members it Has." CNBC, Feb. 17, 2017.

Haselton, T.: "I Tested Amazon's Super-Cheap Microwave That You Can Talk to, and It's Pretty Darn Good." CNBC, Nov. 14, 2019.

Hass, R.: *Twentieth Century Pleasures: Prose on Poetry*. Ecco Press, 2023.

Healy, J.: "It's 4 A.M. The Baby's Coming. But the Hospital Is 100 Miles Away." *The New York Times*, Jul. 17, 2018.

Heggeness, M., Fields, J., Garcia Trejo, Y.A., Schulzetenberg, A.: *Tracking Job Losses for Mothers of School-Age Children During a Health Crisis*. U.S. Census Bureau, Mar. 3, 2021.

Hensel, A.: "As Victoria's Secret's Star Wanes, the Lingerie Market is Growing More Fragmented." *Modern Retail*, Feb. 25, 2020.

Hill, A., Wooden, J.: *Be Quick—But Don't Hurry: Finding Success in the Teachings of a Lifetime*. Simon & Schuster, 2001.

Hill, L., Artiga, S.: "COVID-19 Cases and Deaths by Race/Ethnicity: Current Data and Changes Over Time." *Kaiser Family Foundation*, Aug, 22, 2022.

"How It Works." WellnessFX.

"How Many Products Are Sold on Amazon.com – January 2017 Report." *ScrapeHero*, Jan. 5, 2017.

"Ivermectin and COVID-19." U.S. Food & Drug Administration, Apr. 5, 2024.

Japsen, B.: "Health On-Demand Attracts $1B in Investments." *Forbes,* Feb. 2, 2016.

Japsen, B.: "IBM Watson to Buy Truven Health for $2.6 Billion, Bolsters Data Cloud." *Forbes,* Feb. 18, 2016.

Jhonsa, E.: "Amazon Is Pulling Out All the Stops Against Apple and Google in the Voice Assistant Wars." *The Street*, Mar. 25, 2017.

Johnson, D.: *Tree of Smoke: A Novel*. Picador, 2008.

Jordahl. E.: "The Balance Sheet Bridge." Kaufman Hall, May 13, 2023.

Jurnecka, R.: "Mulally's Testimony Emphasizes Ford's Goal of Fuel Efficiency, Cost Cutting." *MotorTrend*, Dec. 4, 2008.

Kaufman, K., Bates, M., Clarin, D., Fromberg, R.: "Amazon and One Medical: What's Going on Here?" Kaufman Hall, Jul. 27, 2022.

Kaufman, K., Swanson, E.: "Management of Labor in Trying Financial Circumstances." Kaufman Hall, Jul. 28, 2023.

Kaufman, K.: "A Clear and Present Disruption." Kaufman Hall, May 10, 2016.

Kaufman, K.: "America's Hospitals Need a Makeover." Kaufman Hall, Jun. 14, 2023.

Kaufman, K.: "COVID-19 and Black Lives Matter Lay Bare the Need for Healthcare Change." Kaufman Hall, Jul. 13, 2020.

Kaufman, K.: "'Culture Eats Strategy for Breakfast' But Probably Not Right Now." Kaufman Hall, Aug. 30, 2023.

Kaufman, K.: "Getting Culture Right." Kaufman Hall, Nov. 10, 2021.

Kaufman, K.: "Healthcare Costs Post-Pandemic: A Different Perspective." Kaufman Hall, Apr. 7, 2021.

Kaufman, K.: "Healthcare's Wicked Problems." Kaufman Hall, Apr. 26, 2023.

Kaufman, K.: "Hospital Strategy and Planning in Times of Financial Challenge." Kaufman Hall, Aug. 7, 2023.

Kelleher, K.: "Ford Prepares for Mass Layoffs After Losing $1 Billion to Trump's Trade Tariffs, Report Says." *Fortune*, Oct. 10, 2018.

Kelly, J.: "Klarna's AI Assistant Is Doing The Job Of 700 Workers, Company Says." *Forbes*. Mar 4, 2024.

Kerr, D.: "Uber Wants to Be 'the Amazon of Transportation,'" *CNET*, Sept. 6, 2018.

KFF COVID-19 Vaccine Monitor. Kaiser Family Foundation.

Khan, L.M.: "Amazon's Antitrust Paradox." *The Yale Law Journal*, Jan. 2017.

Kim, E., Farr, C.: "Amazon Has a Secret Health Tech Team Called 1492 Working on Medical Records, Virtual Doc Visits." CNBC, Jul. 27, 2017.

Kim, E.: "Amazon Just Made Thousands of Books Free for Its Prime Members — Here's a Simple Reason Why." *Business Insider*, Oct. 6, 2016.

Kim, E.: "How Amazon CEO Jeff Bezos has inspired people to change the way they think about failure." *Business Insider*, May 28, 2016.

Kimbrough, J.: "Every Black Head Coach in the History of The NFL!" ROAR Detroit, Feb. 4, 2022.

Lanier, J.: "How to Picture A.I." *The New Yorker*, Mar. 1, 2024.

"Leading e-Commerce Websites in the United States as of June 2021, Based on Number of Monthly Visits." Statista, Jun. 2021.

Lee, J.M., Hirschfeld, E., Wedding, J.: "A Patient-Designed Do-It-Yourself Mobile Technology System for Diabetes." *Journal of the American Medical Association*, 315(14), April 12, 2016.

Levy, N.: "Amazon Reveals Flurry of New Devices as Tech Giant Aims to get Alexa Inside Homes and Cars." GeekWire, Sept. 20, 2018.

Levy, S.: "DoorDash Wants to Own the Last Mile." *Wired*, Nov. 9, 2015.

Livingston, S.: "Anthem's New Outpatient Imaging Policy Likely to Hit Hospitals' Bottom Line." *Modern Healthcare*, Aug. 26, 2017.

Lombardi, D.: "How a Stanford Professor Helped Lay the Foundation for this 49ers Era." *The Athletic*, Jan. 17, 2024.

Lovelace Jr., B.: "Moderna CEO Says the World Will Have to Live with Covid 'Forever.'" CNBC, Jan. 31, 2021.

Maani, N., Galea, S.: "COVID-19 and Underinvestment in the Public Health Infrastructure of the United States." *The Milbank Quarterly*, Jun. 2020.

Maheshwari, S., Friedman, V.: "Victoria's Secret Swaps Angels for 'What Women Want.' Will They Buy it?" *The New York Times*, Jun. 16, 2021

Mangalinden, J.P.: "Why Amazon's Fire Phone Failed." *Fortune*, Sept. 29, 2014.

Masterson, L.: "UnitedHealth Sees Membership, Revenue Up in Q1." *Healthcare Dive*, Apr. 17, 2018.

McLachlan, S. "35 Instagram Statistics That Matter to Marketers in 2024." HootSuite, Nov. 21, 2023.

Moiel, D., Thompson, J.: "Early Detection of Breast Cancer Using a Self-Referral Mammography Process: The Kaiser Permanente Northwest 20-Year History." *The Permanente Journal* 18(1), Winter 2014.

Morrissey, J.: "When the Waiting Room Is Your Living Room." *The New York Times*, Feb. 24, 2019.

"Most Popular Social Networks Worldwide as of April 2024, Ranked by Number of Monthly Active Users." Statista, 2024.

National Health Expenditures 2017 Highlights. Centers for Medicare & Medicaid Services, 2017.

National Hospital Flash Report Summary: March 2021. Kaufman Hall & Associates, 2021.

Naughton, K.: "Ford to Slash $14 Billion in Costs Under New CEO." *Bloomberg*, Oct. 3, 2017.

"New Census Data Show Differences Between Urban and Rural Residents." U.S. Census Bureau, press release, Dec. 8, 2016.

Newcomb, D.: "Car Tech Startup Investment Exceeds $1 Billion In 2016." *Forbes*, Jan. 27, 2017.

"NFL Releases Statement Slamming Aaron Rodgers' Vaccine Comments." Today Show (via YouTube), Nov. 7, 2021.

Norris, L.: "How to Choose the Best Health Insurance Plan." *Very Well Health*, Mar. 6, 2024.

Odei, B.C., Seldon, C., Fernandez, M.: "Representation of Women in the Leadership Structure of the US Health Care System," *JAMA Open Network* 4(11), Nov. 9, 2021.

"Old Navy Democratizes the Shopping Experience for Women of All Sizes With BODEQUALITY." Gap Inc., Aug. 18, 2021.

Ollove, M., Vestal, C.: "Public Health Systems Still Aren't Ready for the Next Pandemic." Stateline, Jan. 27, 2021.

Oppel Jr., J.A., Gebeloff, R., Lai, K.K.R., Wright, W., Smith, M.: "The Fullest Look Yet at the Racial Inequity of Coronavirus." *The New York Times*, Jul. 5, 2020.

Optum: Overview." UnitedHealth Group

Oremus, W.: "Alexa Is Losing Her Edge." *Slate*, Aug. 23, 2018.

The Pat McAfee Show, Nov. 5, 2021.

Peebles, A., Hirsch, L.: "Amazon Shakes up Drugstore Business with Deal to Buy Online Pharmacy PillPack." CNBC, Jun. 28, 2018.

Pflanzer, L.R.: "UnitedHealth is Already the Biggest US Health Insurer. Now It Wants to Make Going to the Doctor Its Next $100 Billion Business." *Business Insider*, May 31, 2019.

Potter, A., Ward, M., Natafgi, N., Ullrich, F., MacKinney, A., Bell, A, Mueller, K.: "Perceptions of the Benefits of Telemedicine in Rural Communities." *Perspectives in Health Information Management*, Summer 2016.

Priddle, A.: "Mark Fields Out as Ford CEO; Replaced by Jim Hackett." *MotorTrend*, May 22, 2017.

QuickFacts LaSalle County, Illinois; Clatsop County, Oregon; United States. U.S. Census Bureau, accessed Feb. 21, 2019.

Quits Levels and Rates by Industry and Region, Seasonally Adjusted. Bureau of Labor Statistics, May 1, 2024.

Radcliffe, J.R.: "Hoo Boy, There is a Lot of Social Media Reaction Following Aaron Rodgers' Comments on COVID-19 Vaccine." *Milwaukee Journal Sentinel*, Nov. 5, 2021.

"Raymond Cattell." Harvard University Department of Psychology website.

Raynor, G.: "Dawn Staley 'is Philadelphia': Stories from the City That Loves Her Back." *The Athletic*, Apr 7, 2024.

Report to the Congress: Medicare and the Health Care Delivery System. Medicare Payment Advisory Commission, June 2018.

Ricks, T.E.: *The Generals: American Military Command from World War II to Today*, Penguin Books, 2013.

Robeznieks, A.: "Physicians protest harmful Anthem emergency care coverage policy." American Medical Association, Aug. 7, 2017.

Robinson, L., Fitz, T., Goetz, K., Seargeant, D.: *2018 State of Cost Transformation in U.S. Hospitals and Health Systems: Time for Big Steps*. Kaufman, Hall & Associates, 2018.

Roose, K." "Can Ford Turn Itself into a Tech Company?." *The New York Times Magazine*, Nov. 9, 2017.

Rosman, K.: "At Cosmopolitan Magazine, Data Is the New Sex." *The New York Times*, Apr. 5, 2019.

Rural America at a Glance: 2018 Edition. United States Department of Agriculture, Economic Research Service: Economic Information Bulletin 200, Nov. 2018. (Older-age counties are those with 20 percent or more of the population aged 65 or older.)

S. 1130 (115th): Rural Emergency Acute Care Hospital Act, May 16, 2017.

Saad, L., Wigert, B.: "Remote Work Persisting and Trending Permanent." Gallup, Oct. 13, 2021.

Sachdev, A.: "NorthShore CEO Ready to Fight Regulators—and He's Been There Before." *Chicago Tribune,* Jan. 8, 2016.

Sage, A., Lienert, P.: "Ford Plans Self-Driving Car for Ride Share Fleets in 2021." *Reuters*, Aug. 16, 2016.

Saporito, B.: "Boeing Made a Change to Its Corporate Culture Decades Ago. Now It's Paying the Price." *The New York Times*, Jan. 23, 2024.

Scutts, J.: "Helen Gurley Brown: Cosmo Editor's Quest for Glamour, Sex and Power." *The Guardian*, Jun. 8, 2016.

Senge, P.: *The Fifth Discipline: The Art & Practice of The Learning Organization*, Doubleday, 2006.

Shook, N.: "Packers QB Aaron Rodgers Tests Positive for COVID-19, Will Not Play in Week 9 vs. Chiefs." NFL, Nov. 3, 2021.

Singal, J.: "A 15-Year-Old Came Up with a Really Smart Invention for Keeping Alzheimer's Patients Safe." *New York Magazine,* Sept. 19, 2014.

Skogsbergh, J., Woods, E.: "Reorienting Healthcare." Kaufman Hall, Nov. 14, 2018.

Smith, B.: "UConn Head Coach Dan Hurley, 'The Competitor.'" *Sports Illustrated*, Mar. 27, 2023.

Smith, C.: "Roche Acquisitions Continue." *Front Line Genomics,* Aug. 20 2015.

Stevens, L.: "Amazon's New Microwave: 'Alexa, Please Defrost My Chicken.'" *The Wall Street Journal*, Sept. 20, 2018.

"The State of Artificial Intelligence." *CB Insights*, Apr. 11, 2017.

Stone, J.: "UnitedHealth Group Soon to Be Largest Employer of Doctors in the US; Clinical Laboratory Outreach More Critical than Ever Before." *Dark Daily*, Jun. 29, 2018.

"The Story of Netflix," Netflix.com.

Strogatz, S.: "One Giant Step for a Chess-Playing Machine." *The New York Times*, Dec. 26, 2018.

"Survey: Hospital CEOs See Digital Innovation as Critical, But Significant Roadblocks Remain." AVIA, press release, Sept. 21, 2017.

Tabuchi, H.: "How CVS Quit Smoking and Grew into a Health Care Giant." *The New York Times,* Jul. 11, 2015.

Teasdale, B., Schulman, K.A.: "Are U.S. Hospitals Still 'Recession-proof'?" *New England Journal of Medicine*, Jul. 1, 2020.

Templeton, A.: "With Too Many Patients and Too Few Colleagues, Oregon Nurses Say: 'We're Drowning.'" Oregon Public Broadcasting, Sept. 6, 2022.

Terhune, C.: "Anthem to Buy Cigna for $54 Billion, Creating Nation's Largest Insurer." *Los Angeles Times,* Jul. 24, 2015.

"Tesla Hits a New Milestone, Passing G.M. in Valuation." *The New York Times*, Apr. 10, 2017.

"Thoughts on the Business of Life," *Forbes*.

Tracer, Z.: "Centene to Buy Health Net in $6.3 Billion Health-Care Deal." *Bloomberg Business*, Jul. 2, 2015.

Trends in the Use of Telehealth During the Emergence of the COVID-19 Pandemic — United States, January–March 2020. Centers for Disease Control and Prevention, 2020.

Tully, S.: "CVS Wants to Make Your Drugstore Your Doctor." *Forbes*, May 17, 2019.

Unequal Treatment: What Healthcare Providers Need to Know About Racial and Ethnic Disparities in Healthcare. National Institutes of Medicine, Mar. 2020.

"United Health Group Inc. (UNH) CEO David Wichmann on Q2 2018 Results – Earnings Call Transcript." *Seeking Alpha*, July 17, 2018.

"UPMC Announces $2B Investment to Build 3 Digitally Based Specialty Hospitals Backed by World-Leading Innovative, Translational Science." UPMC, Nov. 3, 2017.

Velazco, C.: "Netflix Learned How to Stream Good Video on Bad Connections." Engadget, Mar. 1, 2017.

Vena, D.: "12 Years Ago Steve Jobs Introduced the iPhone, and Everything Changed." The Motley Fool, Apr. 15, 2019.

Verlaine, J. , Benoit, D.: "JPMorgan, Goldman Call Time on Work-From-Home. Their Rivals Are Ready to Pounce." *The Wall Street Journal*, Jul. 6, 2021.

Vlasic, B.: "Ford Installs a New C.E.O." *The New York Times*, May 22, 2017.

Walter, M.: "ACR: Anthem's New Outpatient Imaging Policy is 'Arbitrary,' 'Unwise.'" *Radiology Business*, Aug. 29, 2017.

Watkins, M.D.: *The First 90 Days: Proven Strategies for Getting Up to Speed Faster and Smarter*. Harvard Business Review Press, 2013.

Weber, L., Barry-Jester, A.M.: "Most States Have Cut Back Public Health Powers Amid Pandemic." Associated Press, Sept. 15, 2021.

Wingfield, N.: "Amazon's Cloud Business Lifts Its Profit to a Record." *The New York Times*, Apr. 28, 2016.

Wolken, D. "UConn's Dan Hurley is the Perfect Sports Heel. So Kentucky Job Would be a Perfect Fit." *USA Today*, Apr. 9, 2024.

Wong, N.C.: "The 10,000-Hour Concept." *Canadian Urological Association Journal*, Sept.-Oct. 2015.

Yala, A., et al: "Multi-Institutional Validation of a Mammography-Based Breast Cancer Risk Model." *Journal of Clinical Oncology*, 40(16), Nov. 12, 2021.

Zeitchik, S.: "Is Artificial Intelligence About to Transform the Mammogram?" *Washington Post*, Dec. 21, 2021.

Zimmerman, J.: "Rodgers Controversy Dominates Talk on Local Sports Radio." WBAY, Nov. 5, 2021.

.